The New Global History

Bruce Mazlish

 Routledge
Taylor & Francis Group

NEW YORK AND LONDON

First published 2006 by Routledge
270 Madison Ave, New York, NY 10016

Simultaneously published in the UK
by Routledge
2 Park Square, Milton Park, Abingdon, Oxon OX14 4RN

*Routledge is an imprint of the Taylor & Francis Group,
an informa business*

© 2006 Bruce Mazlish

Typeset in Sabon by RefineCatch Limited, Bungay, Suffolk
Printed and bound in Great Britain by
TJ International Ltd, Padstow, Cornwall

British Library Cataloguing in Publication Data
A catalogue record for this book is available from the British Library

Library of Congress Cataloging-in-Publication Data
Mazlish, Bruce, 1923–
 The new global history / Bruce Mazlish.
  p. cm.
 Includes index.
 1. Globalization—History. I. Title.
 HF1359.M388 2006
 303.48′2—dc22
 2006011007

ISBN10: 0–415–40920–9 (hbk)
ISBN10: 0–415–40921–7 (pbk)
ISBN10: 0–203–96894–8 (ebk)

ISBN13: 978–0–415–40920–9 (hbk)
ISBN13: 978–0–415–40921–6 (pbk)
ISBN13: 978–0–203–96894–9 (ebk)

Contents

Acknowledgments

A topic of this size places its author in debt to many people. Only some of those to whom I owe inspiration and help in various ways, in the course of working directly on the subject for over a decade and a half, can be acknowledged here. Among my many colleagues in the field whom I would like especially to thank are Michael Adas, Nayan Chanda, Raymond Grew, Akira Iriye, Krishan Kumar, Elliott Morss, Wolf Schafer, and Dennis Smith. In addition, there are three reviewers of the original MS from whose suggestions I benefited, and I wish to express my appreciation to them. To numerous others not mentioned by name I convey my apologies.

For assistance on particular points, I would like to thank Lester M. Salomon and Helmut Anheier. Kate Bigger has been of inestimable assistance in helping me with the computer on which the MS first came to life, as well as in other ways. For the formatting, which then morphed into general editorial assistance, I am grateful to Ken Weisbrode, whose own involvement in the global history project has been steady and sustaining.

The footnotes are intended to serve as a sort of bibliography, although citing many works not usually to be found in the standard lists. In these footnotes, additional evidence of my debt to many particular persons can also be found.

Two of the chapters appeared earlier in different versions, and I am obliged to the original journal publishers for permission to reprint portions. One is "The Hijacking of Global Society," a version of which appeared in the *Journal of Civil Society*, vol. 1 (2005), pp. 5–17. Reprinted by permission of Taylor and Francis Journals, http://www.tandf.co.uk. A version of "The Global and the Local" appeared in *Current Sociology*, vol. 53, no. 1 (2005), pp. 93–111. Portions of that article are reprinted by permission of Sage Publications Ltd, Copyright (© International Sociological Association/ISA, 2005). It was a pleasure to work with both journals and their editors.

Vicky Peters, the editor at Routledge, not only accepted the MS initially, but also secured the proper reviews and then supported the book through the entire editorial process (while having a baby at the same time). I offer my appreciation as well to Vicky's supporting staff, Eve Setch, Philippa Grand, and Emma Langley.

Neva Goodwin, my wife, has played so many roles in the conception and nurturing of this book that she deserves multiple thanks—all of which I gladly tend her, with much love. In her own right she is a professional economist, but one who doesn't lose sight of the big picture. Thus, she played a critical—indeed, she is my most constant critic in the best sense of that term—role in my writing this book, both on the small and the large scale.

Introduction

This book is a critical inquiry into the present-day process of globalization. The inquiry is guided by an interdisciplinary perspective, in which the historical is central. It is also guided by the desire for impartial scholarship and empirical research, which is then connected to theory. Such a stance generally is antagonistic to a passionate partisan position, but here I am conjoining the two. I do so for two reasons: scholarship that pretends to be without passion is a charade—the passion exists although it may be carefully concealed from both the reader and the scholar him/herself. And, second, I believe that our understanding and actions—that of leaders and general public alike—today are sadly out of joint with the process of globalization taking place, with dire consequences as a result.

The chapters that follow seek mainly to illuminate the process of globalization taking place around us, so dangerously ignored by the "statesmen" who need to be setting policies to deal with it. This is especially true when we realize that we are on the cusp of a period in which, while nation-states still prevail, their sovereignty and boundaries are being challenged and transcended. As a preliminary definition of globalization, we might offer at this point the following. It comprises a set of historical changes that are leading to an ever higher degree of interdependence and interconnectedness. A consciousness of these changes is widely shared around the globe, as is an awareness that they are affecting human experience, in varying ways, in every part of the globe. Although many of these changes were set in motion a long time ago, the consciousness that gave them a name and a shared reality only became widespread in the 1970s.[1]

The lack of real information about the parts, or what could also be called elements, but which I prefer to call factors, of this process is matched only by the amount of misinformation concerning them. Similarly, the lack of historical depth in most attempts at dealing with the subject is often appalling. This lack is compounded by Cyclopean vision in which parts are mistaken for wholes and holism is a non-existent word and practice. While there are many brilliant and astute analysts and observers of globalization, many policy recommendations are often based on thin historical and empirical foundations. Theory and data are neglected. The resultant generalizations suffer accordingly.

Having said this, I am aware that I run the risk of myself over-generalizing. In general, a curse of work in the field is the tendency not only to over-generalizations but to black-white characterizations—for example, we are told globalization is simply imperialism under a new name. I do not wish to tumble into such Manichean divisions. Still, I am struck by the nebulous state of knowledge about what is undoubtedly one of the foremost features of recent history, an increased globalization. The term can readily be seen as a "key word," in the sense made famous by Raymond Williams, of our contemporary world.

At which point many historians and other social scientists might say that this is all very well, but if globalization is a familiar feature of other times, why insist on its newness today? After all, one can root the globalization process in prehistoric times, when hunter-gatherers roamed the world. One can focus on its manifestation in more historic times: the Silk Road of the early Middle Ages, the New World explorations of the early modern period, and so forth. The answer is that not to recognize what is new in the global-ization that sets in some time after World War II is to commit the error of substituting the search for earlier precedents and origins—emphasizing that there is nothing totally new under the sun—for an analysis and study of contemporary phenomena in their proper context.

Amidst much confusion, it is clear that great anxiety surrounds both the process that is going on around us, and the study of that process. Where are the archives, ask the historians? Why are we wasting time looking at non-economic factors, ask the economists, convinced that globalization is simply the extension of the free market? And why bother promoting the study of a process that is so destructive of peoples and the environment, ask the anti-globalizers?

In another dimension there are those historians and social scientists who subsume what is happening under the label of world history, with global history as its synonym, and refuse to acknowledge that something different has emerged in the last half of the twentieth century, which then causes us to look back and redefine what is meant by global history. And yet another way of dismissing the new phenomenon is to label it contemporary history, which as everyone knows is too recent to be studied properly.[2]

New Global History (NGH), the name taken to set off the study of present-day globalization from previous manifestations of the process, has been reluctantly embraced by some of my colleagues and myself as a necessary demarcation of inquiry. Indeed, the line between New Global History and Global History is still not itself fast. What matters is the recognition that something important has happened in the last fifty years or so, and as we head into the new millennium, and that this requires a new openness and a new mindset if we are to understand it well enough to grapple with it effectively.

(1)

In what follows, I attempt to deal in detail and depth with many of the issues adumbrated above. Problems of periodization and dating come front and center. Discriminations of the new approach in comparison, say, to that of world history require elaborations. Mostly, however, in the chapters of this book I try to deal with what I am calling the factors of globalization, those elements that comprise it and illustrate both the causes and the effects of increased interdependence and interconnectivity. In a sense, factors are the new or newly important actors that need to be studied in detail. Multinational corporations (MNCs), the non-governmental organizations (NGOs), the United Nations, to name a few, pose problems of research for us, to be undertaken in the framework of NGH and its emphasis on synergy, synchronicity, and holism.

Some repetition will be required in some of the chapters, to remind us of the framework in which our research proceeds. While trying to keep the repetition to a minimum and to present the repeated material in as fresh a light as possible, I also recognize that repetition has its own virtue in an enterprise that is seeking to break new ground and to cross established boundaries of thought and of discipline.

The social science disciplines that arose in the aftermath of the French and Industrial revolutions have been of great value in professionalizing the way people think about the major problems of the society of the last few centuries. Their power and significance should not be underestimated when I add that today many of them have become obstacles to understanding the phenomena, encapsulated in the term globalization, that surround us. Such phenomena have broken down many of the old boundaries in our daily lives, boundaries that are still perpetuated, however, in the disciplines. Moreover, the disciplines have frequently become ideologies as well as bodies of knowledge. As an instance, one only needs to look at neo-classical economics, which is the ideology par excellence of the free market underlying much of the push to globalization.

NGH, as remarked, given the present state of the professional demarcations, is vigorously interdisciplinary. It may also mark the incipient breakdown of existing disciplines. If so, new or modified ones will only emerge over time, in the doing. The one thing of which we can be sure is that, just as the nation-state must be reexamined in the glare of globalization, so must the existing social science studies. Reexamination does not mean discarding them but refining and changing them, a task for future social scientists. No wonder globalization arouses such strong feelings of anxiety and a sense of risk. It requires us to set out for a new land—should we say space?—of experience and knowledge. The chapters that follow are intended to be *mappa mundi*, initial guides to the terra and spatial incognitos that lie somewhere beyond our present knowledge.

(2)

In addition to chapters on the perspective required for the understanding of present-day globalization, on the framing of the subject, on its problems of dating and periodization, on the version of history to be used in these endeavors, and on factors such as the MNCs, the NGOs, and, perhaps surprisingly, the Cold War, I want to argue that the most neglected, though probably the most long-range and important, aspect of our subject is to be found in a changing consciousness. Out of the synchronicity and synergy of factors studied in the chapters of this book a global consciousness is emerging as a matter of practice, not just wishful thinking or ideal aspiration. Often it is accompanied by a new identity, a global one. This identity is taking shape gradually, and it both displaces and adds to the more local ones with which we are already struggling.

There are clear policy implications of the view I am advancing. As I said at the beginning, scholarship requires as much impartiality as possible in the doing, but legitimately eventuates in commitment to certain political positions. Knowledge does have meaning, and does not exist simply for its own sake. For example, in the chapter on "The hijacking of global society," I try to exemplify this belief in concrete form. Plunging into the current debates about Islam and American Empire, I seek to place the discourse in the context of globalization seen historically.

Lastly, I take up the question of morality and globalization. There seems to be relatively little consideration in the literature of this topic, despite its importance.[3] In three chapters on different ways into the subject, I try to open it up, inviting others to follow. It's a bit like being the first person on a cross-country run, breaking the track, or so I feel. My first foray is to consider the respective weight of the global and the local as we try to make moral cum political decisions, and to argue that the former, i.e., the global, has much to recommend it (though balance must be maintained as we pursue this track). The next chapter takes a closer look at the possibility of a "higher morality" and what its conditions might be. This then leads to a third chapter, examining Humanity as the constituency for political, social, and moral decisions. After these chapters, a brief conclusion brings factors of globalization, moral and policy considerations, and Humanity together.

Such is the vision put before us by the practice of New Global History, as a way of understanding our increasingly interconnected existence.

Part I

Nature of New Global History

Chapter 1

Globalization without end

A framing

Let us start with two ways of looking at globalization. The first assumes that globalization is a thread running through all of humanity's past, starting with generations of our hunter-gatherer ancestors, over millennia, gradually migrating across the world. In this sense, there is no set beginning, as well as no foreseeable end. The second involves the fact that globalization in its present-day incarnation is a subject of endless debate as to what it is and where it is going. Taken together, these two ways add up to a kind of "globalization without end," both as discourse and possible reality.

In the Introduction, I essayed a brief definition of globalization. It is well to go a bit further now with this problem. Many who brush up against this definitional problem are aghast at the lack of agreement on what the term means, and often throw up their hands and mutter under their breath "globaloney." This understandable frustration is misguided. Any concept used in regard to large-scale social processes is bound to be vague and contested, for it seeks to aid us in grasping powerful and protean forces, twisting and turning over time, and not easily encompassed by words. So the first thing to recognize, as one scholar tells us, is that "the meaning of some concepts derive [sic] from controversy rather than from any consensus about their meaning."[1]

It is essential to recognize that globalization's meaning or meanings lies in the very arguments brought to bear on the concept. In its simplest form, I will argue, it is a theory about social relations, emphasizing that those relations, whatever their specific form, are becoming more widespread, with the parties to them more and more interconnected and interdependent in various ways. There is always a geographical dimension to this development as greater expansion into the world takes place. Without all parts of the world becoming more and more known, there can only be a limited increase in social relations. In speaking of geography, I should add that today's virtual space is as much a dimension of interconnectivity as was the sixteenth-century circumnavigation of the globe or any number of other, similar transformations of geocultural space.

To give a bit more support to this kind of definition, I will cite the historian

C. A. Bayly's view that globalization is "a progressive increase in the scale of social processes from a local or regional to a world level."[2] For him the concept is a heuristic device, one that draws attention to dynamics, while abjuring a description of progressive linear social change. Thus, his definition has the merit of suggesting to us a difference between global, or new global, history and what is called world history; the latter tends to deny or neglect directionality. In contrast, accepting the idea of direction in historical development, the sociologist Sylvia Walby speaks affirmatively of globalization as "a process of increased density and frequency of international or global interactions relative to local or national ones."[3] With these additional definitions, we are on our way to a focused concern with present-day globalization as studied by new global historians.

(1)

Though my emphasis will be on the new globalization, we must constantly bear in mind its antecedents and earlier forms, even at the risk of reciting well-known facts (although they are placed in a new light). Central to the globalization of the past few centuries has been the state, or rather the nation-state. Indeed, as has been frequently noted, the transcending of nation-state boundaries is at the core of one variation on the definition of globalization. Consequently, the coming into being of the modern state is an essential feature as we try to understand globalization past and present.

After the Treaty of Westphalia in 1648, a governmental structure that emphasizes sovereignty becomes more and more important.[4] A brief description suggests that such sovereignty is both political and economic, for the modern state functions increasingly as a single market. Additionally, in theory, such a state is to respect the inviolable sovereignty of other states, but in practice resort is often had to war. Such wars require ever more efficient tax systems, military technologies, improved communications, and a host of similar devices, and thus the further strengthening of the state.[5]

All of these developments can also be found in empires. What was new in the modern states that arose in Europe was their acceptance in principle of other sovereignties, whereas empires, at least according to Martin Van Creveld, cannot accept equals. As he puts it, empires "looking beyond their borders . . . saw not other political communities with a right to an independent existence, but barbarians."[6] With nation-states, moreover, we have the possibility of an international system, made up of equal sovereignties along with laws and conventions by which they adjust their relations to each other, and settle differences peacefully. Before the nation as such we cannot really have an international system.

There is a vast literature on the nation-state. I have drawn on it here to make the point that without its emergence what we call globalization today, especially as it plays out in regard to internationalism, would have no meaning. So, too, the European state has been the prime agency in the exploration of the globe, and in its subsequent exploitation. It is the state that introduced the era of global warfare, with the War of the Spanish Succession (1701–14) anticipating the world wars of the twentieth century. It is the nation-state that has been cloned globally (even with only partial success), with over 190 of them now represented in the United Nations. In short, an early phase of globalization was carried out by the very form, the nation-state, which is now under subversion by present-day globalizing forces.

(2)

That is one part of the earlier globalizing story. Another piece is the rise of merchant empires. Their primary aim was to pursue profit, though this might entail the use of violence. In this they differed from the nation-states that stood behind them, which had territorial gain as a direct goal and assumed violence as the necessary means of such acquisition. The two, state and merchant empire, go together, however, for it was the relatively small and rivalrous states, for example, Portugal, Spain, the Italian city states, the Netherlands, England, and France, whence the merchants and their ships came and went, West and East.

It was, as we know, primarily as a result of the new states and the merchant empires that a quantum jump took place in the fifteenth century, and the whole globe swam into view. We need not rehearse the discovery of the "New World," the subsequent circumnavigation of the globe by Magellan in 1517–20 and the later voyages of discovery in the Far East, but merely signal their role in this early phase of globalization. A nice symbolic touch is afforded by the present of a magnificent golden globe whose oceans were made from green enamel by Francis Drake to his Queen, Elizabeth, after being knighted for his circumnavigation of the globe in 1580—the first by an Englishman—and his plundering of the Spanish fleet.

Central to the whole story is the sea. Covering about seven-eighths of the earth's surface, it stood outside the usual empires of history, an uncharted and unconquered realm. When the small nations of the West built fleets that could sail upwind, they could open a new chapter in history and reach all parts of the globe, with the Atlantic and the Pacific oceans linked through the Straits of Magellan. No wonder that "stout Cortez" (actually, Balboa) stood in awe, as Keats tells us, at the sight of the Pacific glimpsed from a peak in Darien!

Numerous advances in astronomy, mapping, surveying and navigating were required for the European vessels to find their way across the largely uncharted seas. As it turned out, navies were expensive, and most empires had neither the will nor the means to harness their resources in this direction. Those states that did profited greatly, though paying a terrible price in lives lost to the watery depths. In any case, the future lay with the European control of the oceans. Spurred on by a religion claiming global dominion— the papal demarcation of most of the known globe between Spain and Portugal was a palpable demonstration though in the event unsuccessful— and by a market-driven economy that knew no geographical limits, the European powers gradually and painfully established a global hegemony. These European nations, becoming imperial, merged the national and the global in one sweeping movement.

The effect of the merchant empires was both material and cultural. As one scholar puts it, "Silks and cottons, coffee and tea, tobacco and opium, tomatoes and potatoes, rice and maize, porcelain and lacquerware—the impact . . . on European material culture proved profound and permanent. No less striking were the mental changes, beginning with wonder at strange plants, beasts, and men, and culminating in the fruitful cultural relativism that spouted from European encounters with Americans, Africans and Asians."[7] It is not too much to claim that the merchant empires, along with developments in science and philosophy, helped create the conditions in the seventeenth century that led to the early Enlightenment and all that follows from that, including the sense of cosmopolitanism.

Such is the European perspective. In the eye of global history we must also see the impact of the merchant empires not only on their home countries, but also on those whose shores they reached. Japan can serve as one example. In the sixteenth century, Japan and, in this case, Portugal were initially ignorant of one another, as if existing on separate planets. When a vessel carrying a small band of Portuguese merchants was blown off course and three of its men landed in the southwest of Japan, each side was significantly affected by the encounter. The Europeans encountered a culture more civilized than their own, while the Japanese were made aware that "there is another world greater than ours."[8] Such effects were confirmed by the English who arrived in Japan almost 60 years later. Though the Westerners had superior astronomy and knowledge of navigation, they were struck by the sharp swords of the samurai and the cultivated aesthetics of their Japanese hosts. On the Japanese side, muskets and cannon were briefly incorporated by the Shogun into his army, helping him to establish the Tokugawa power that was to persist until the second opening of Japan, with Perry's arrival in 1853, when the Tokugawa was succeeded by the Meiji regime.

These are global effects. They are part of the connections being made by the expansionist powers of Europe through their mastery of the seas. They also mark the beginnings of the gulf of superior development that was to open up between the West and the rest of the world, a development which is conceived of as going forward under the banner of modernity. In this effort, the state and its merchant empires were joined at the hip. The resultant globalization was part of nation-building, in which emerging nations were achieving supremacy over existing empires, or rather substituting ocean-based merchant empires for more traditional land-based ones.

From the beginning, it was trade that played the major role in the great change in awareness that underlay this phase of globalization. It was economic exchange, carried out by the merchant empires, that dramatically affected the conceptualization of space, which, along with time, stands at the heart of one decisive definition of globalization. Of course, there were other causes underlying the great expansion and, paradoxically, contraction of space/time. But the merchant empires are the prime carriers of that change in coordinates. Subsequent history can be told as the story of that ever-increasing contraction and expansion.

It is in this light that we should think of America. America, of course, was supposed to be China when Columbus set sail for the fabled East. Once the new awareness that it was a separate continent took hold, America became the scene of national/imperial expansion in the Southern part, with Spanish conquistadors as agents of the state. In the North we find our familiar merchant empire, embodied in such groups as the Hudson Bay Company and later the Massachusetts Bay Company. Thus, America, as it became known, accidentally being named after Amerigo Vespucci, and with the North subsequently arrogating to itself that name as if South and Central America did not exist, was global in its inspiration, with its discovery affirming the fact that a globe existed, to be circumnavigated shortly thereafter.

Collapsing a long story, I want simply to underline the fact that America became part of an empire, the British one, intimately tied to the merchant empires that traded in slaves, and thus of the entire plantation base of the early modern economy. Henceforth, race would haunt the history of the future USA, a "local" effect of a global movement. So, too, Africa was dragged into the globalization that characterizes this phase of development, though subsequently falling behind Europe and Asia in terms of both nation-building and modernity. In short, as American historians are coming gradually to realize, we cannot understand the USA any more than other sections of the world without placing it from the beginning in the context of globalization.

(3)

I want momentarily to expand our panorama before narrowing our attention to the present and its new globalization. Humanity has sought to give meaning to its existence in time and space through many means, myths and religions being prime examples. With the coming of a form of knowledge known as "history," arising in "scientific" form, i.e., as promulgated by Herodotus and Thucydides in fifth-century Greece, universal or world histories arose. Such visions took the form not only of universal history, but more recently of philosophies of history, world-system analysis, world history, Big History, Global, and now New Global History.[9]

Clearly, there is much debate as to the nature of globalization, its origins, its nodes of existence, how it might be studied, and so forth. One important contribution is the book *Globalization in World History*, edited by A. G. Hopkins, which deals with some of the early stages of global history. A collection of essays, it attacks the illusion that globalization is simply a Western creation, and argues that it is a state of affairs jointly created by all parts of the world. The essays give details about Asia, Islam and other areas and cultures, and their participation in the construction of globalization, though the focus is much on the eighteenth century and the role of the West. In addition, Hopkins sets up a schema in terms of archaic, proto, modern, and postcolonial globalization, best viewed, however, as a "series of over-lapping and interacting sequences rather than as a succession of neat stages."[10] Hopkins' collection and its ideas serve as a useful transition to the New Global History as well as to the discussion of present-day globalization that I am undertaking in this book.

(4)

In undertaking this task, I want to emphasize anew the holistic nature of our enterprise. To do so is to stress that, as one author commented about coloni-alism, an early factor in modern globalization, it is simultaneously a "pro-cess in political economy and culture . . . indissoluble aspects of the same reality."[11] Or rather, I would argue, globalization is a matter of politics, economics, cultures, and many other factors—reflecting the synthesis and synergy mentioned earlier—a whole that we break into parts because of our inability immediately to grasp it entirely, as well as for disciplinary reasons. That is why, to deal with this problem, New Global History is so insistently interdisciplinary. This is why the sort of analysis involved in the work, say, of Kevin O'Rourke and Jeffrey Williamson, who claim the period 1870–1914 was marked by greater globalization than the present, is so narrow, limited to economics, and resolutely ignoring the larger context in which this one part of globalization exists.[12] It is for this reason that we need a new perspective, embodied in what I am calling New Global History, building as it does on the World and Global histories that have come before it.

In the simplest terms, then, New Global History is dedicated to the study of the new globalization that has emerged some time in the period after WW II. Revealing is the entry of the word "globalization" into the human vocabulary. Some argue that it was coined in the 1960s in the USA or in Latin America, others that it is a neologism introduced in the 1970s by the Japanese. Whichever is correct—and more research is needed on this topic— it represents a profound shift in human consciousness, symbolic recognition and thus self-awareness of what has been taking place in real life. The term speaks of an historically unprecedented development, as part of which the national, regional, and international are supplanted or supplemented by global forces. These are not under the control of any government, and are best spoken of in terms of flows and processes. They present problems that can no longer be dealt with adequately on the local level, but require global efforts.

Not surprisingly, present-day globalization is not only new and emergent, but incomplete and unequal in its effects, good and bad. For scholars it gives rise to what Arjun Appadurai has called "anxiety" about globalization studies. Where, they may ask, are the archives from which to write its story? How can it avoid the pitfalls of self-proclaimed contemporary history (although it is now more than 50 years old) where we are too close to events to understand them? One way to deal with such anxiety is to dismiss the phenomenon completely: it's nothing new, only old wine in new bottles. Another way is to pour scorn on the subject by calling it a mere fashion, soon to pass away. A more dramatic way is to embrace anti-globalization and try to reverse the process itself, whether by protests (such as against the World Trade Organization and World Bank), boycotts (e.g., against Nike), or other demonstrations of hostility.

Closely connected to such scholarly anxiety is the notion of risk. Thus it is the thesis of Ulrich Beck and others that today we are faced with "global, often irreparable damage that can no longer be limited."[13] This can take the form of global warming, ozone holes, disease spread by air travel or acts of human destruction for which no insurance can compensate. Unlike natural disasters, these risks result from "decisions that focus on techno-economic advantages and opportunities and accept hazards as simply the dark side of progress." In a global epoch, of course, these consequences may be both irreversible and catastrophically affect the entire world.

Add to anxiety and risk a host of misperceptions and one can see readily why globalization is such a contested term. As noted earlier, many see present-day globalization as a teleological and deterministic process whose outcome is a homogenized world on the model of America. This flies in the face of the evidence for increasing heterogeneity and the multiculturalism that characterizes many of the developed countries. In similar vein, there is the charge that globalization is simply another word for imperialism. Again, the evidence suggests that, as my historical presentation attempted to show, colonialism and imperialism were partial causes of the earlier globalization that took place before the 1950s, and that present-day globalization may have strong imperial components in it, as the recent discussions about empire suggest, but that a simple equation is ridiculous. In any and all such controversies it helps, too, if we can remember that almost by definition present-day globalization is not just Western but a jointly created process not under any one state's control but made what it is and will be by many agents.

(5)

With these brief comments, I come to a caesura of sorts in my account in this chapter of globalization without end. Of course, each and every factor involved in present-day globalization has antecedents and a genealogy of some kind in back of them. They are involved synergistically and synthetically with one another, and it is the interplay of all the factors that makes for a concept usefully called new globalization. And it is this, in turn, that gives rise to a new global history to study it. What I am suggesting here, however, is that new globalization and its history can only be understood properly in the light of previous surges of globalization and attempts to study their emergence and subsequent trajectories.

It need hardly be remarked that I have scanted or left out completely in my account so far many aspects of the new globalization. (I shall touch on some of these in the Conclusion.) A host of topics requires specific attention. There is, for example, the need for comparison with other such idols of abstraction as cosmopolitanism, colonialism, imperialism, civilizations and empires. As a protean process, globalization can hardly be dealt with without engaging in what seems like unlimited intellectual warfare.

Should we be surprised that such "warfare" has become increasingly global in scope? That almost nothing seems left out of our discussions? That every part of the world is now engaged in a global discourse? That terms like multiculturalism, postmodernism, hybridity, creolization, and so forth flow freely around the world? The fact is that, for better or worse, globalization has become the hegemonic word of our era, inserting itself into all aspects of our lives and our efforts to understand them. Our task, of course, is to break the concept into its parts, and then both to study the parts empirically and to conceptualize them anew into an understandable and manageable whole. It is a seemingly endless task, but one suitable for a globalization that, for the moment at least, seems without end.

Chapter 2

Onwards and outwards

A kind of revolution

As all of us, especially historians, know, there is nothing completely new under the sun. In writing about global history, or rather the new global history, I am aware that I am following a path on which others have taken steps, sometimes giant steps. Let me touch on a few of my predecessors.

I start my tale with Adam Smith and Karl Marx. It was Smith who truly revolutionized economic thinking by emphasizing the division of labor and its promise of almost endlessly increasing production. Its only limit, as he announced in Chapter 3 of *The Wealth of Nations*, was the extent of the market. Building on Smith's perception, Karl Marx, in the *Communist Manifesto*, described how "Modern industry has established the world-market, for which the discovery of America paved the way." His following analysis is uncanny in its anticipation of what is occurring today in the process of globalization (to highlight this fact certain words have been italicized in the quotations from him). Modern industry for Marx, of course, is directed by the bourgeoisie. In sonorous phrase after phrase, Marx hymns the accomplishments of that class in expanding the market. "The need of a constantly expanding market for its products chases the bourgeoisie over the whole surface of the globe. It must nestle everywhere, settle everywhere, *establish connections everywhere*. The bourgeoisie has through its exploit-ation of the *world-market* given a *cosmopolitan character* to production and consumption in every country." And one more quote: "The bourgeoisie, by the rapid improvement of all instruments of production"—here Marx added technology to Smith's division of labor—"by the immensely facilitated means of communication, draws all, even the most barbarian, nations into *civilisation*."

One forgets too often that Friedrich Engels was the co-author of the *Manifesto*; he has always been in Marx's shadow. However, in preparation for the great document of 1848, Engels had written a year earlier, in his "Principles of Communism," that: "A new machine invented in England deprives millions of Chinese workers of their livelihood within a year's time. In this way, big industry has brought all the people of the earth into contact with each other, has merged all local markets into one world market, has spread civilization and progress everywhere and has thus ensured that whatever happens in civilized countries will have repercussions in all other countries."[1]

One more of the oracular voices must be heard. It is Max Weber's, as when he introduces his *Protestant Ethic and the Spirit of Capitalism* by announcing that "in Western civilization only, cultural phenomena have appeared which (as we like to think) lie in a line of development having *universal* significance and value." Weber then briefly discusses some of these phenomena, including science, and concludes that "the most fateful force in our modern life" is capitalism. Marx had spoken of the capitalist's "werewolf appetite" for profit. In more somber tones, Weber wrote that "capitalism is identical with the pursuit of profit, and forever *renewed* profit."[2] Then he explains its dynamism in less animal-like terms than those used by Marx, stressing its multicausal nature, and especially emphasizing its rational aspect.

It is astonishing how portentous the words of Smith, Marx, Engels, and Weber have turned out to be. They seem to have recognized some of the forces of globalization—science, technology, capitalism—in their early manifestations and sensed their future implications. Even lesser men caught what was in the air, where solid structures were melting. Thus, in the debate over the Napoleonic Code of Commerce in 1803, a proponent of one clause in the Code exclaimed, "The bill of commerce has been invented. In the history of commerce this is an event almost comparable to the discovery of the compass and of America . . . [I]t has set free movable capital, has facilitated its movements, and has created an immense volume of credit. From that moment on, there had been no limits to the expansion of commerce other than those of the globe itself."[3]

Yet, it is one thing to acknowledge premonitions about globalization, and another to recognize that what is going on around us today transcends these earlier conceptualizations of the phenomenon, though building on them.[4] Before turning back to our own effort to deal with the subject, one last quotation on the particularly economic nature of globalization. It comes from Manuel Castells' *The Rise of the Network Society*. There he announces that: "The informational economy is global. A global economy is a historically new reality, distinct from a world economy. A world economy, that is an economy in which capital accumulation proceeds throughout the world, has existed in the West at least since the sixteenth century, as Fernand Braudel and Immanuel Wallerstein have taught us. *A global economy is something different: it is an economy with the capacity to work as a unit in real time on a planetary scale*" [my emphasis].[5]

(1)

Up to now I have been standing on the shoulders of tall figures, if not giants. It is time to get down and start trudging on the path they have laid out. In doing so, I am, as acknowledged earlier, practicing a form of contemporary history. A further word in defense of my practice. Whether consciously we admit it or not, our writing of history is, overtly or covertly, in part an attempt to situate ourselves correctly in regard to current problems. So it is in regard to our effort to understand globalization today. While employing a multidisciplinary approach, we must comprehend that process in a wide-ranging historical perspective. In doing so, we help create what will become our own past, is now our present, and is unfolding before us as our future.

The fact is that we are entering upon a global epoch.[6] That is the revolutionary development of our present time. Unlike other revolutionary efforts at global reach, such as the communist, the forces of globalization do not have to take on political form. Rather than seizing state power, they are, in fact, often undermining existing state powers. While states do remain major actors in the global epoch, power is shifting increasingly to amorphous forces, such as environmental, or to communications networks, or to new, less fixed sorts of institutions, such as multinational corporations and non-governmental organizations.

This is the major transformation through which we are now living. To signal its importance, we do not need to adopt an apocalyptic tone, nor assume that it will be a linear and completely deterministic development. The "event" itself, occurring as we enter a new millennium, speaks everywhere for itself. What we do need, however, is to raise our awareness—our consciousness—to the level of our situation.

In order to help achieve that sense of new global history and a greater consciousness of our present situation, it is necessary to describe and analyze some of the major features of the emerging global epoch. In this aspiration, I am taking up anew the burden of the classical sociologists, only now on a more extended plane. The classical problem in social theory had been to explain the transition to "modern" society. Marx, preceded by Adam Smith and Hegel, sought both to describe and to analyze the tremendous transformation from "feudal" to "modern," the shift from a society based on personal relations to one largely based on impersonal market forces. Where Marx focused on the economic relations of production, his later compatriot Max Weber emphasized the new rationality. Others stressed cultural factors, and still others highlighted the role of science and political power.

Now the transition to be described and analyzed is not to industrial society as such, but to the globalized society in which increasingly all peoples live. Indeed, the very term "epoch" marks from the first a global perspective. It came into general usage in the early nineteenth century in the field of geology, where the new science was seen as addressing the entire earth.

Geological processes were viewed as worldwide. As William Buckland, one of the pioneers in the new field, remarked, "The field of the Geologist's inquiry is the Globe itself."[7] One spoke, for example, of the Eocene Epoch, marking a new and important period in the earth's development (or, as the change in regard to the earth's flora and fauna would be called after Darwin, evolution). Such an epoch was necessarily global in its dimensions.

Periodization of any kind is central to the human effort to organize time (whether human or geological). We impose boundaries on the otherwise chaotic happenings of the past, seeking to order them by restrictive names. Decades, eras, centuries—these are alternate divisions to that of epochs. Of course, such orderings can, on occasion, mislead rather than guide us through the chaos of events. So, too, can the larger periodizations of Western history: the famous ancient, medieval, modern divisions. We may take for real what is only an illusory reification of time.

This is the test that the phrase "global epoch" will have to undergo. On the assumption that the phrase holds up meaningfully, it offers us an escape from the rather clamorous modern–postmodern debate. With the notion of global epoch, I am suggesting that we have an alternative way of revising, or renewing, our sense of history. In short, the most useful, i.e., illuminating, successor to "modern" history as a periodizing rubric is, I believe, global or "new global history."

(2)

The historical, of course, is simply one way of looking at phenomena. It does have the potential, however, of offering the longer view, and of thus providing a depth of understanding to its object of study that is otherwise unavailable. To recapitulate, globalization can be looked at primarily as an economic development, e.g., as a stage of late capitalism. It can be viewed as a mainly political development, where the nation-state is seen as the prime actor losing vital functions. Or the focus can be on the cultural changes, with a presumed homogenization occurring among peoples. With its holistic approach, of course, New Global History seeks to both integrate and sift through these various ways of looking at the phenomenon.

History's conceptual weakness is that it must deal with all the aspects of a phenomenon—e.g., economic, political, cultural—and the ways they interrelate, yet without an overall, satisfactory theory as to how that interrelation takes place. Yet, its weakness is also its strength, for it is the only one of the human sciences that at least attempts to understand the full, complex reality of human behavior over time, even if under-theorized. To compensate, it must draw heavily on the other human sciences, and their theories and approaches.

History, i.e., historiography, is itself subject to the forces of globalization. For most of human "history," i.e., the 99 percent of the species' past as hunter-gatherers, recorded history, the conscious attempt to know the past "scientifically," did not exist. It is a late development in human evolution. Whether one chooses to start this development with the ancient civilizations of China or India, or wishes to argue for its true beginnings with the Greeks a few thousand years ago, it is clearly of comparatively recent vintage.

Starting perhaps in the seventeenth century, a Western mode of "scientific" history achieved prominence and power. It also achieved hegemony, imposing its Eurocentric version on other peoples. As E. H. Carr innocently expressed the initial stage of this happening, "It is only today that it has become possible for the first time even to imagine a whole world consisting of peoples who have in the fullest sense entered into history and become the concern, no longer of the colonial administrator or the anthropologist, but of the historian."[8] Chinese scholars now look at their past with the same scholarly methodology as found in the West; Indian scholars do the same. In the process, of course, they are changing the Eurocentric myopia, and enlarging all humanity's historical perspective. A new global history, therefore, is possible, though indubitably starting from certain Western preconceptions as to how one conducts such a study.

In short, the practice of history is itself necessarily undergoing globalization. In so doing, it becomes a subject to be studied just as we do other parts of the phenomenon. The very perspective then, the historical, that is used to study globalization is not a static one, but subject to shifting forces and fates. Hence, the lens by which we look at the globalization process becomes itself part of that very process. How exactly this regrinding will occur, only time—and the practice of new global history—will tell.

(3)

In further seeking to understand globalization, especially from an historical perspective, we run into a number of problem areas. A major one concerns the actors to be studied. For the last few hundred years, the writing of history has circled around the activities of the nation-state, its wars, its economic activities, its nationalistic culture, and its political leaders. Profound shifts are underway in this regard. Though, as I have argued, the nation-state will still be a major player in New Global History, its role must be reassessed in terms of the larger process unrolling around it.

At the same time, other players than the nation-state crowd the stage of history. Especially prominent, as we have noted, are multinational corporations (MNCs) and non-governmental organizations (NGOs), both of whose increase in numbers recently has been phenomenal. In a fuller treatment, some of which I will provide in the next section of this book, we would wish to consider their emergence in relation to the notion of civil society, tracing the latter's growth in the soil first laid down in the Enlightenment cultivation of the public sphere and public opinion.

Here, however, I want to focus in a preliminary way on two prominent forms of NGOs, those related to human rights and to the environment. Human rights is a global assertion, rising above the national rights restricted to citizens by earlier democratic movements. Today, although this view is hotly contested in some quarters, one has rights not because one is a German, Frenchman, Iranian, or an American, but because one is a human being. As we all know, however, there are few if any institutionalized "global" courts to enforce these rights (though they are enshrined in a UN Declaration). It is the court of public opinion that mainly gives whatever strength there is to their observation.[9] And that public opinion is shaped and given voice by NGOs, such as Amnesty International, Human Rights Watch and other such organizations. In other words, in our informational/computer age, human rights proponents, in the guise of NGOs, are to a large extent the self-appointed conscience of the globe.

Another proliferating form of NGO relates to the environment. In this area, private, not-for-profit groups mobilize on both a local and a global basis to deal with threats to ecology. It is such groups that prod national governments to take international actions, and advise international agencies how to go about doing this. Using the new informational technology, NGOs such as the Sierra Club, Greenpeace and innumerable others mobilize forces around the world to combat what are clearly global as well as local crises.

Turning now to multinationals, as our other selected actor, they have been traced back two thousand years by classical scholars.[10] This is accurate in the sense that certain trading groups operated across political boundaries. It is anachronistic in that nation-states did not exist at the time, thus giving a different meaning to multinational. When we add the word "corporation," we again must realize that that is a legal term given precise meaning only recently. In any case, modern multinational corporations can be discerned emerging in the seventeenth century and flourishing, for example, in the shape of the Dutch and British East India companies.

Eschewing a continuous history, let us jump to our global present. Today, according to the UN, of the 100 largest possessors of Gross Domestic Product (GDP) over 50 are multinationals. Which means that they are wealthier on that index (which, in fact, can be misleading, confusing value added with GDP; symbolically, however, it is on target) than about 120 to 130 nation-state members of the UN. Another figure: today there are said to be over 60,000 multinationals, a dramatic increase over the numbers existing only a few years previously. And yet another figure: in the past quarter of a century, the list of the top 500 industrial multinationals has shifted from almost entirely American/European to almost two-fifths Japanese/Asian.

How are we to understand what is happening? As a preliminary, we necessarily must define what we mean by a multinational corporation. Then we must describe and analyze the features that we think characterize it: where is it headquartered? Where is its workforce? Where are its sales?

Where go its capital flows? etc. Then we must look at these features dynamically, seeing them develop over time. Then we must compare companies with companies and countries with countries, arriving at a global picture.

In fact, an international conference, as part of the New Global History initiative, took place in October 1999 to undertake exactly these tasks. Called "Mapping the Multinational Corporations," the project sought to give visual form to what is happening economically on our globe. To complement the atlases featuring nation-states and their boundaries, it has compiled an atlas, *Global Inc.*, depicting the multinational corporations as they leap across such boundaries.[11]

Increasingly, then, it is the multinational corporations along with the NGOs and an adapting nation-state that are the actors to be studied by the historian or other social scientist. Alongside of these forces, of course, must be placed the UN. A cross between a forum for nations, with their pursuit of national aims by international means, and an institution seeking to transcend its members and their parochial concerns, the UN is still unsure of its mission. That mission, it dimly senses, is a global one, but how to move to fulfill it is clouded in ambiguity and dissent. Justice and Force would seem to be the two key terms in this regard: how to adjudicate local power squabbles in global terms, which must include prevention, and how to enforce UN judgments militarily are the clear challenges. For the student of globalization, the evolution of UN military forces deserves all the attention he or she can give it.[12]

(4)

At this point, we may feel somewhat overwhelmed. There is such a plethora of problems to be found in the seemingly simple notion of globalization. Are we to take everything as our object of study? In one sense, the answer is "yes"; globalization, as I have stressed, must be seen holistically, for each feature is connected to every other. Realistically, however, we can ignore huge swathes of ordinary history and concentrate initially on the factors of globalization, some of which I have tried to enumerate. Doing so, our tasks become limited research projects. Only gradually do we seek to reassemble the pieces, in turn further illuminating our empirical research efforts.

Nevertheless, it is evident that globalization as a real phenomenon threatens to overwhelm us, as does the attempt to conceptualize it. Even the name is contested. Alternative terms for globalization are globalism, glocalization, and globaloney, all of which speak for themselves to one degree or another.[13] Perhaps even more importantly, globalization must be recognized as coming before us not only as an idea, or concept related to a process, but as an ideology, promoted by multinational corporations and by various media, and as an ideal, a new version of the brotherhood and sisterhood of humankind. In short, everything about the subject must be assumed to be a *problematique*.

For by now it must be clear how complicated the subject of globalization is, and how an understanding of the process is so vital to our sense of where we are and how we have come to be there—wherever "there" is. In truth, globalization has redefined, and reoriented, as I have argued, our coordinates of space and time. Here on earth we now have a feeling of a "full earth," in the sense not only of our everywhere encountering other peoples, but in the sense that almost all of the planet's surface and increasingly its depths are becoming known to us. Such knowledge is being matched by our invasion of space, formerly seen as "empty" and "outer." But such "outer" space, in turn, is being increasingly drawn inward, as we reorder our sense of self on earth in terms of the new knowledge we are acquiring.

That knowledge tells us that fundamental economic, political, social, and cultural changes are taking place in a global fashion, in the process we call globalization. Difficult as it is to pin down, and correlated as it is with profound scientific and technological developments, a revolutionary transformation in consciousness, in self-consciousness, and in historical consciousness has been and is taking place. This, in fact, may be the most important consequence of the globalization process. In sum, we are not only transforming the globe but ourselves as well.

Part II

Factors of New Global History

Chapter 3

Cold War and globalization
Unintended consequences

Present-day globalization is the result of many factors interacting with one another. Some observers look upon this result as foreordained, a teleological outcome. Others, and I number myself among them, see globalization as an unintended, yet logical, consequence of powerful forces all pushing in a discernible direction toward greatly increased interconnection and interdependence of peoples and societies.

In seeking to date the coming of globalization—or, really, new globalization, for, as we have seen, there have been previous episodes that could claim the name—much depends on the weight one gives to the various factors. Thus, a case can be made for new globalization starting in the 1950s, or the 1980s, or even the 1990s. What I think is incontestable is that while consciousness of globalization arose with the term, which appeared to emerge first in the 1960s, there are strong grounds for believing that the process itself must be viewed as arising initially during and post-World War II. With that granted, what I want to argue here is that the forcing house of globalization is to be found not only in the 1939–45 war, but also in the Cold War that succeeded it.

(1)

World War II, coming after World War I, was even more global in its nature than its predecessor. Its operations covered almost all parts of the world, even if in unequal fashion. The philosopher Karl Jaspers perceived this fact presciently in 1955, when he wrote: "It was the Second World War which first accorded full weight to the contribution from everywhere, to the globe as a whole. The war in the Far East was just as serious as that in Europe. It was in point of fact the first real world war."[1] Thus the conflict of 1939 to 1945 served as an anticipation of some of what was to come under the later heading of globalization; it is a forerunner in military dress of the mobilization of the entire globe in a singular struggle.

There were many other important implications for globalization emerging from WW II. As a result of the Nazi horrors, the judicial road to international justice was broadened via the Nuremberg trials. Here the momentous shift from war crimes to crimes against humanity was made. Genocide was declared the defining feature. Genocide, however, was a limited operation. More important for the emerging globalization was the reification of people into Humanity, a transcending concept befitting the new world being created. People live in territories. Humanity is an abstraction whose abode is necessarily global. Henceforth, a constituency existed in ideal form—Humanity—whose coincidence with the globalization process was self-evident, and in whose name "local" decisions could be judged.[2]

The war also meant the destruction of Germany and Japan as great military powers, paving the way for the emergence of a bi-polar world made up of the two superpowers, the Soviet Union and the USA. None of this would have been possible, of course, if the world had still been divided up into areas dominated by the Axis and Allied powers. But with the field of competing states simplified, a major step could be taken toward a more unified world—once the Cold War ended with the removal of one of the superpowers. Needless to say, this was a long-drawn-out process, and was not really settled until 1991. But at that point, in principle, there was only "One World," with different countries having different weights to place in the scale of power, but that power exercised in a world that was global in nature.

First, however, there had to be the Cold War, to settle which of the superpowers would prevail. Their visions of the coming one world were very different. The Soviet version was construed in old-fashioned international terms—after all, Marxism was modeled on an International of the workers. Its success was presumably foreordained, as communism would spread by virtue of its superiority to a dying bourgeois order. Eventually, it would penetrate to all parts of the globe. There was no "plot" of expansionism, though the Soviet Union was not loath to push where it could. It could, however, or so it believed, afford to be patient, for History was on its side. In fact, the vision of the future unified world held by communists was vague. In the meantime, there were competing contestants—China as well as Russia, for example—as to who would lead the way to that utopia.

On the other side, the US pursued a strategy of containing the Soviets worldwide, while seeking to establish in the areas under its control a "free world" built on a "free market" and democratic institutions. The idea specifically was to rebuild Western Europe, which was done by means of the Marshall Plan, and thus to pin it on the side of the free world. Japan was to be so included by other means. Both were then to function, democratically, in an economic system, operating in terms of the Bretton Woods agreement and a number of international organizations, such as the World Bank, the International Monetary Fund (IMF), and the World Trade Organization. Nominally free, a closer look shows that this entire system was largely dominated by the USA.[3]

Whatever America's intentions, however, the world began to spin out of its control. Favored by the economic aspects of globalization, pioneered and led by the United States, the glimmerings of a global civil society emerged during the 1960s and 1970s. Once the US perceived this emergence, it began to throw its weight against it, leading to the later rejection of Kyoto, the land mines treaty, the International Criminal Court, and other such initiatives.[4]

Nevertheless, as we can now see, it was the Cold War struggle between two superpowers in the midst of a process of globalization that became the *sine qua non* for the continuation of that process. In 1940, at the beginning of World War II, Wendell Wilkie ran for president on the Republican ticket, on a platform of "One World," the name of his book. He was unexpectedly prescient. Though it took a number of decades during which the world was semi-globalized, i.e., split over the competing visions of the Soviet Union and the USA, the end result was indeed a one world of sorts, created in the image of the American dream. As it turned out, however, little recognition was given by American administrations to the fact that the world had changed and become global. Or, when dimly aware that the ideological pursuit of the free market had helped create something new and different, resort was to be had to an American Empire rather than a global society.

(2)

We need now to go into greater detail and to retreat a bit in our thinking, going back to World War II and then the Cold War as the cradle of globalization. During World War II itself, two new technologies were developed with major implications for the transcending of national boundaries. One, of course, was the development of nuclear weapons. With the bombing of Nagasaki and Hiroshima, a force was introduced into the world with the potential to destroy all or most of humanity. Clearly, its use overstepped traditional boundaries and left the nation-state in the position of being unable to defend itself against this threat. Even a "local" use of nuclear in the form of energy could erupt past lines on the map, as was illustrated by Chernobyl, and "invade" its neighbors. Nuclear technology, in short, was by nature a global force.

Equally significant was the development of rockets during the war, especially at first by Germany. After hostilities ceased, these quickly led to the development of missiles (which, of course, could carry nuclear warheads) and to the exploration of outer space. When "Mankind" launched itself beyond the planetary atmosphere, it embarked upon a revolutionary step that had both philosophical and practical consequences of enormous importance. In terms of philosophy, it meant that, at the most extreme, *Homo sapiens* had become, so to speak, a new species. If a lion acquired wings, would we not classify it as a new species? With human beings, of course, we don't think in this way; yet it is not clear why we should not. The main reason we do not in fact do so is that human beings, unlike the mythical lion we have conjured up, can take off their "wings" and put them on again. Evolving into a prosthetic god, the human remains the same at the same time as "it" evolves.[5]

More easily graspable is that the step into space has fostered a new consciousness. As we look back from the space craft in which we are speeding to the moon, we see the blue planet behind us as "spaceship earth," as R. Buckminster Fuller put it. Airplanes before this had allowed us to see portions of the earth from on high. Only out in space, however, can we actually see the full earth, spinning in its orbit, as we orbit far above it. This is a global vision, and enhances the consciousness we have of how globalization requires a changed mentality. Like the implied species change spoken of earlier, this philosophical development is a late product of what had happened during the war of 1939–45.

With the mutation of that war into the Cold War of the succeeding years, both nuclear and ballistic missile development proceeded apace. The coming of the hydrogen bomb, the launch of Sputnik, the US response, and the leapfrogging that took place subsequently in these areas meant a weapons race that increasingly was fought out in terms of space—outer space. Such space transcended the national sovereignties involved and has to be thought of more and more as global. In this view, "World" War II recedes into a local happening that is largely a preliminary to the spatial expansion of conflict that we call the Cold War.[6]

Two other technical developments are central to the emergence of the present-day globalization process. One is the lofting into the sky of satellites, foreshadowed by Sputnik. These made possible an enormous compression of space-time, so that real-time exchanges became possible, superseding anything previously accomplished by telegraph, telephone, or radio. Again, the impact on consciousness was deep and pervasive even when unconsciously so. More immediately, the satellites, allowing for instantaneous communication, greatly facilitated the growth of MNCs and NGOs. Both exhibit a lift-off after World War II that takes the shape of a J curve, as we will see in more detail in later chapters. Both, of course, are defining agents in the globalization process with which we are concerned.

Add to this the development of computers, the so-called computer revolution. Although already foreshadowed in the nineteenth-century work of Charles Babbage and his difference engine, the development took a quantum jump in the course of the world war (for example, in terms of encryption devices) and especially in the immediate aftermath. Financed by the US Defense Department, under the heading of ARPANET, which went on-line in 1969, this development became the seedbed for the establishment of the World Wide Web and the global network it makes possible. ARPANET, in fact, was an accident, in the sense that the military felt it had to have decentralized computer facilities, with the unexpected result that the computer networks were "free."[7]

(3)

Much of what I have just spoken about concerns technology or technology-related developments that made possible greater globalization. Other factors are more political. One of great importance is anti-colonialism. World War II made the assertion of independence by former European colonies feasible in a new way. Quick to take advantage of the situation was, for example, India, followed rapidly by Indo-China, and then Algeria, to name just a few. This breakdown of empire was called by General George S. Marshall a "world revolution," and so it was.[8]

The end of colonial status for many peoples was requisite for a global world of juridical equals. (In reality, of course, some nations were more equal than others.) It allowed for a United Nations that grew from 60 or so nations to around 190 at the turn of the millennium. Before going on further about that development, let us stick with decolonization. This last must be linked to the emergence of what was called the Third World. Though I have been speaking about a bi-polar world preceding a One World, during the Cold War of the superpowers an intermediate space seemed to open between them. The result, of course, was fierce competition between the Soviet Union and the USA for their allegiance. Each decolonized country was seen as a military base to be denied to the rivals in the superpower conflict, or as a source of raw materials, such as oil. Only with the end of the Cold War and the US triumph has the notion of a Third World faded away. In the resultant globalized world it has been replaced by a North–South divide. Such a divide, however, takes place in a One World or facsimile thereof.

Before leaving this aspect of our subject, we need to recognize that the war taking place during the 1950s to 1980s was "cold" only in regard to the two superpowers. In fact, a "hot" war raged on non-US or Soviet soil consisting of about 149 localized wars, resulting in about 23 million deaths. It is these wars that led some, including the Mexican Subcomandante Marcos, to argue that the Cold War should be renamed the "Third World War," fought out by the superpowers in that third part of the globe.[9]

Yet another part of the Cold War struggle saw the projection of military power in terms of American bases in Germany, Japan, and South Korea, to be matched by the Soviets in Eastern Europe, Cuba, Angola, and other places. Another piece of the puzzle wherein we discern the dismantling of a bi-polar into a single world has to be the impact of this competition on the Soviet Union, contributing to its demise. A case can be made that the Soviet Union, geared as it was to an industrialized world, could not make the transition to an information society.[10] This failure contributed to the move to a greater globalized world than the one that had helped undo the Soviet empire.

The markers on that decline and fall can be seen in the Helsinki Accord of 1975, and the subsequent proliferation of NGOs in Eastern Europe, the rise of Solidarity, and so forth, all features of the expanding globalization process. Or at least aided by it. While clearly so momentous a development as the collapse of communism in the Soviet Union cannot be explained in terms of single-factor causality, the pressure of globalization must be recognized as an essential element.

(4)

In history's strange movements we can also glimpse how the Soviets' invasion of Afghanistan in 1979 was both part of its Cold War rivalry with the USA and a major contributing factor to the rise of a post-Cold War version of globalization: Global (or Globalizing) Islam. As can be seen, particular decisions have general consequences. The Soviet move to expand its presence and power evoked an American response. The US decided to support and arm radical Islamists as they waged a jihad against the spread of Soviet communism in their country. The American move was part of its containment policy, with momentous and paradoxical results.

First, the Soviet side of the matter. Between 1979 and 1989, when the Soviets withdrew in a debacle that undermined its strength at home as much as abroad, hundreds of thousands of Afghans were killed and many millions displaced. Vietnam had been a similar disaster for the USA, but did not effectively call into question the legitimacy of the governmental regime (not the same as the administration) that was behind the debacle. In Russia the case was more extreme; the failed invasion and humiliating retreat were factors in the collapse of empire in Eastern Europe and within two years of the Soviet empire itself. The Cold War was over, the USA the winner.

Paradoxically, however, the victory was pregnant with future battles and threats. With the Soviets gone from Afghanistan, the Taliban took over. The jihadists now became America's Frankenstein, picking up where the Soviets had left off in their opposition to globalization in the form of "Western" values, power, and influence. Fundamentalist Islam now asserted itself as a global contender. Its jihad fighters, having honed their skills in Afghanistan, turned their attentions more and more not just to the Middle East but to the whole world. In fact, as globalization fostered migrations of Muslims into the Western countries, they were perceived by some as an internal threat, a kind of Trojan horse. The US, drawn into Afghanistan, but now with its own forces as well as its Afghan alliances, has become responsible for providing security to over 25 million people—and to nation-building (that it has been doing this badly and irresponsibly does not alter the fact).[11]

Meanwhile, local jihad has turned into global jihad. Osama bin Laden's

Al-Qaeda has morphed into other shapes and with other leaders. Its follow-ers' destruction of the World Trade Center in New York in 2001 carries great symbolic meaning, as well as wide-ranging security and economic costs, not to mention the way in which the death and destruction gave new life to the otherwise declining fortunes of the George W. Bush administra-tion. The consequences of 9/11 are far-ranging and only briefly glimpsed at the moment. We must settle here for a simple pointer to what must be studied carefully and in detail (in Chapter 6 we go a bit further in examining parts of the phenomenon). What can be seen clearly is how the Cold War helped spawn a new variant of globalization, Global Islam, one that now interacts with all the other factors of the new globalization being produced after World War II.

(5)

Having been diverted, via decolonization, the appearance of a Third World, the impact of globalization on the Soviet Union, and, finally, the Soviet inva-sion of Afghanistan leading to the unexpected fostering of Global Islam, we can now return to the UN as it emerges from World War II and into the period of the Cold War. As I have remarked, from the beginning the organ-ization has had a split personality. It was the creature of sovereign nations, whose sovereignty it was to protect from aggression, and thus ensure a peaceful world. In this aspect of its being it was a continuation of post-World War I's dedication to inviolable nation-states, all theoretically gathered in a League.[12] As such the UN is an international organization, not a global one. It has another side, however, manifest in the Declaration of Human Rights. Its preamble speaks of peoples, not states. Its mandate to protect humanity encourages the UN when necessary to "violate" national sovereignty. Thus, the Declaration points the organization in a global direction.

The UN, of course, also became the site of the Cold War contestation. The Soviet Union and the US both tried to control the votes of the so-called non-aligned states, most of them newly decolonized, and to influence "world opinion" by incessant maneuvering over votes and positions increasingly oriented to globalizing tendencies. Neither was prepared to give up its veto in the Security Council (nor were the other three members), nor any erosion of what it took to be its sovereign national rights. Yet, inexorably it seems, the pressures involved in the Declaration of Human Rights and in various agencies of the UN pushed the globalization process forward.

Thus, the UN, a product of World War II and a site of contestation in the Cold War, must be numbered among the numerous factors we have been noting as fostering the globalization process. It almost seems as if everything—technological and economic developments, national and inter-national decisions, movements of consciousness—was moving, in to and fro fashion, toward a single end. This is misleading in many ways—little or none of this was intentional—but it does add up as if to a predetermined pathway. As I remarked earlier, one must be careful and not mistake tendencies for teleologies, nor a present development for an assured one. One must be equally careful, however, not to miss the drift of events.

In earlier centuries, appeal was had to God, or Providence, or an invisible hand to explain what I am calling the drift of events. It is worth detouring for a moment to give depth to this idea. Thus, in his *Natural Theology* (1802), the Reverend William Paley wrote: "Those actions of animals which we refer to instinct, are not gone about with any view to their consequences ... but are pursued for the sake of gratification alone; what does all this prove, but that the prospection [that is, knowledge of ultimate benefit], which must be somewhere, is not in the animal, but in the Creator?"[13] Elsewhere, Paley uses the phrase "invisible hand."

We can take this quotation in two directions. One is to Darwin, who read Paley carefully, and who substituted the theory of evolution by natural selection for the Creator, thus leaving us with a secular explanation of how things unfold. In Darwin's story, there is no intention, no teleology, in nature, only the mechanism of survival of the fittest. What direction, if any, this leads in is a matter of much contestation, with some biologists alleging a movement toward greater diversity and complexity of creatures and others denying any such thing. I myself believe that evolutionary theory must be the backdrop for any explanation regarding human behavior, but cannot be directly applied to humans and their historical journey because humans do have conscious intentions.

We must go back before Paley and Darwin for other inspirations as we attempt to understand human evolution. The phrase "invisible hand" takes us to Adam Smith, of course, for his transmutation of this idea into that of market mechanisms—laws of supply and demand—and to the less precise idea of what he calls the "silent revolution," which brought about the shift in Europe from feudal society to commercial society. It is, as he tells us, the result of peddlers wishing to turn a penny profit, and noblemen bartering away their landed strength in order to purchase baubles and trinkets. Thus an event of the greatest importance was a result of what Smith recognized as the working of the mechanism of unintended consequences.

Even before Smith, a fellow Scotsman, Adam Ferguson, had grasped the idea clearly and forcefully. In his *Essay on the History of Civil Society* (1767), we find a passage such as the following: "Like the winds that come we know not whence, and blow whithersoever they list, the forms of society are derived from an obscure and distant origin; they arise ... from the instincts, not from the speculations, of men. ... Every step and every movement of the multitude, even in what are termed enlightened ages, are made with equal blindness to the future; and nations stumble upon establishments, which are indeed the result of human action, but not the execution of any human design."[14]

One such "establishment," I am arguing, is globalization. It has come about, and is coming about, from human actions, only a small number of which are intentional about global society as an end, but most of which are rooted in other human designs. My argument, therefore, is that globalization is an unintended consequence, which is nevertheless to be understood as the consequence of numerous factors, such as those I have tried to outline above.

One of these factors has been World War II and the Cold War that followed upon it. For many historians war is such an unpleasant fact of life that they prefer to ignore its role in history. Ferguson would have none of this view. In fact, his theory of civil society is predicated on the belief that conflict among nations, including war, is requisite for social bonding and civic well-being. It is animosity that brings about national cohesion.[15] There is much evidence in support of this view, especially in an age of nation-states and more recently the ethnic and religious struggles that swirl around them.

For better and worse, war has been a mother of invention, and of unintended consequences. It is this view that I have been applying to my analysis of the Cold War and globalization. One of the "inventions" emerging from that war has been an intense drift toward globalization, which has as one of its aims the abolition of war as such, with ironically the Cold War as one factor in this drift. If humanity does not destroy itself in the process of pursuing its instinctual ends, one of the paradoxical consequences may well be a profound change in the conditions of human social bonding. In a possible global civil society, other ties than those created by enmity and war with "others" may be in the process of being created. In place of the Creator spoken about in previous epochs we have unintended consequences converging in a particular direction and acting as the *deus ex machina* of the global epoch.

Chapter 4

The multinational corporations
Ruling the globe?

The Cold War is a segment of recent history, usually treated in traditional fashion by historians as an episode in international relations; I have suggested that the Cold War also deserves treatment as a context for the rise of globalization. The appearance in the course of present-day globalization of two major new actors, the multinational corporations (MNCs) and the non-governmental organizations (NGOs), requires a somewhat different treatment. They are actors in the process of globalization, rather more than, as with the Cold War, the complex context in which globalization made its appearance. Needless to say, they did not emerge full-blown from Clio's forehead in the post-WW II period.[1] Both had an existence before present-day globalization in various shapes and forms. Only after 1945, however, do they become preeminent players on the global scale.

As such, they share the stage with nation-states, which continue to be the central actors even in the global epoch. Some commentators see the MNCs as displacing the state in importance. I think it more useful to look at the evolving relationship between the two, and to study the MNCs in their own right (reserving the study of the NGOs for the next chapter). There is, of course, an enormous literature on them, starting with the definitional problem—what is an MNC?—and advancing to the questions of their change over time, their shift in terms of geographical place, their transformation during the process of globalization, and so forth. For example, there seems to be a general shift from trading companies to resource extraction, then to manufacturing, and then to service and financial service companies as the dominating types of MNCs, a shift which is gradual and in which the earlier forms do not disappear but persist as part of a larger whole.

My aim is not to tackle the MNCs per se, but to bring to bear on them the perspective of New Global History. And even here only in terms of a limited optic, more to show how the perspective works than to give a total picture. Specifically, I will treat the MNCs as much more than mere economic actors; their actions have profound impacts on and implications for the rest of society. Even here, however, I will not focus on MNCs in their entirety, which could range from the environment to consumerism and all points in between, but rather on the MNCs in regard to the problem of governance. For they are the new Leviathans of our time, and consequently have great political as well as economic power; indeed, in the eyes of some, as noted, they can claim to rule the world.

I will seek entrance to the realm of MNCs, therefore, by first asking the question: who rules the globe? A simple and clear answer exists to this rather simple-minded question: no one state, party, person (although for the religious minded the answer might be God). This conclusion is especially true in what we are labeling a global epoch or an Age of Globalization. Here we are confronted increasingly with flows and processes, difficult to control or even to understand. These amorphous entities seem to escape the power and authority of existing institutions, and to transcend their restraining boundaries. (Indeed, we can perceive that these amorphous flows and processes pose challenges to the national state as well as to the international system.)

In the fictional universe of the sci-fi writer Isaac Asimov, for example, in his book *I Robot*, a couple of corporations do, in fact, take on the role of ruling the globe. For our part, we need not go to that extreme, but simply examine the actual way in which MNCs have increasingly come to dominate our societies. They are clearly one of the ruling forces in our world, challenging, supplanting, or collaborating with more established institutions, such as the nation-state. As the name multinational suggests, they are still connected to nations, though the nature of the connection has been rapidly changing. In this setting, we need to recognize the MNCs, as suggested earlier, as Leviathans—using the term in imitation of the sovereign state treated by Hobbes in an earlier time—now taking on, potentially or in practice, the power and authority of more traditional structures.

(1)

The importance of MNCs was made dramatically evident in the UN statement, noted above in Chapter 2, that of the 100 largest possessors of GDP over 50 were corporations. In this view, these MNCs are wealthier and thus potentially more powerful than 120 to 130 of the nation-states. Though this measure is, in fact, as previously noted, misleading—the figures given in regard to the MNCs are based on revenue rather than value added, i.e., the way in which GNP is measured—it symbolizes an important truth: when the corporate revenues of a company such as Exxon-Mobil or Wal-Mart are greater than the GDP of a country such as Austria, for example, our traditional conceptions of who rules the world must be closely reexamined.

The simplest definition of an MNC, sometimes also called a transnational enterprise, is a firm that controls income-generating assets in more than one country at a time. A more complicated and meaningful definition would add that an MNC has productive facilities in several countries on at least two continents with employees stationed worldwide and financial investments scattered across the globe.

Taking 1600 as our starting point, we found the English East India Company and its Dutch counterpart, plus a small number of others, as our early examples. Plotting a curve, we see very slow, almost flat, growth through the decades until 1914, when we can number about 3,000. Growth subsequently occurs very gradually until in 1969 we can count 7,258, and then there is an explosion with the curve rising to 18,500 in 1988, 30,400 in 1992, 53,100 in 1987, 59,902 in 1999, and 63,000 at the turn of the century![2]

Aided by technology—improved communication via satellites and other devices, faster transportation, and so forth—the MNCs have grown by leaps and bounds in the process we call globalization. Large and small, coming into and going out of existence with some rapidity, these business enterprises have rushed past national boundaries and transcended existing power relations. While they vary in type—some are state related, for example—most are on the model of the American private corporation. This certainly is so on principle; in fact, of course, there are all kinds of mixed modes. Still, overwhelmingly, they are not public entities, though grounded in public and national law. As many of their CEOs have declared, the primary loyalties are to globalized companies rather than to the countries in which they are headquartered.[3]

The phenomenal growth of the MNCs is marked by increasing concentration at the top, characterized by mergers and acquisitions resulting in huge corporations. We seem to be in a sort of post-Westphalian stage: in the seventeenth and eighteenth centuries this stage was marked by the absorption and disappearance of various political state bodies, i.e., principalities, provinces, and so forth; today a similar process is taking place only now in regard to our new economic Leviathans. Thus, of the Fortune 500 list of a few decades ago, 33 percent no longer existed in their own right ten years later. Fifteen years later, in 1995, another 40 percent were gone. What stands out, however, is the steady persistence of the growth in MNCs and their power.

At this point, we have a relatively nuanced and calculable picture of MNCs and their historical development. Although still sketchy, this picture allows us to return better informed to the question of whether and in what ways the MNCs, with their werewolf appetite for expansion, to use Marx's phrase, are able to translate their economic power into other forms—cultural, political, social—as well. It is to this question that we now turn directly.

(2)

In the broadest sense, the MNCs have an impact on almost every sphere of modern life, ranging from issues of personal identity to issues of community, from policymaking on the environment to international security, and from the future of work to the future of the nation-state, and beyond the state to regional and international bodies and alliances. Impact, however, is not the same thing as controlling power.

The first thing to be said is that MNCs are corporations, that is, legal entities created by the state.[4] In theory at least, the state controls the corporations, can subject them to taxes, and can entangle them in regulations and restrictions. In practice, however, as a result of globalization and its market arrangements, the MNC can often escape these bonds by "rigging" the state, that is, using the corporations' financial strength to "buy" the government apparatus through corruption and campaign contributions. More fundamentally, in its search for low labor costs and favorable tax codes, the global corporation can move its operations in order to escape onerous state controls. In this sense, it is rootless and so amorphous that it cannot be captured by national state institutions. In turn, its currency and market manipulations fall into a vacuum, where no international body has authority. In a word, the MNCs are masterless.

Now it should be clear that this last statement is somewhat hyperbolic; yet it points in the right direction. With this said, however, masterless does not equate with masterful. Indeed, the case can be made that the MNCs are the beneficiaries of a system of institutions such as the IMF and the World Bank that has been set up by states, and specifically the United States. The international financial regime encapsulated in the terms of the Bretton Woods system is, in this view, a prerequisite for the economic and political power exercised by the MNCs as, under the regime's umbrella, they shape the process of globalization. On such a reading, the state and MNCs reign together.[5]

MNCs can influence the state in particular instances, for example, affecting and perhaps determining government policy in regard to nationalistic takeovers, such as Venezuela. Influence is obviously exercised when CEOs shuttle in and out of governments, most egregiously in the USA in terms of the military/industrial complex. Again, however, we must emphasize how general and difficult to grasp firmly such versions of "rule" necessarily are. By themselves, MNCs "rule" only in the most shadowy of fashions. It is as part of a system that they exercise what powers they have. And that system is both a national one and a global one. It is especially, I would argue, in the latter realm that our new Leviathans are most powerful.

Opposition to them also often takes a global form. Worldwide protests and anti-globalization movements are the counterweights to the powers of the MNCs. After all, MNCs sometimes undermine national government efforts to control their own economies, may use foreign investments to dictate dependent governments' actions, can promote consumerism in ways deleterious to the health and welfare of the client nation, and so forth. MNCs can also be accused of tilting the North/South scales further in favor

of the former. Operating on a global scale, MNCs are opposed by global anti-globalists, often with the aid of various international non-governmental organizations (INGOs) and NGOs.

Such opposition is made stronger by the very nature of the MNCs. They are non-representative and non-accountable, or, if they are, only so to their shareholders. As participants in ruling the globe they are not seen as legitimate in part for the reason just given. While themselves sovereign, in the sense of being relatively free from external control, they are hardly transparent as governments are supposed to be. Questions of democratic governance abound. If, in fact, MNCs exercise partial rule in our global society, must they be held to account for their policies and actions, and these be made known to world opinion?

In the strange ways of history, the MNCs have been heavily invested in creating the NGOs, and beyond them the global civil society of which they are a part, and which together hold the MNCs accountable and call their legitimacy into question. In the eighteenth century, economics and trade were seen as constituent parts of civil society. Now, in the view of most theorists, they stand outside that circle. In fact, however, it is the MNCs that have provided the satellites that permit and foster global communication and the computer websites that facilitate the spread of the NGOs and their messages. The devil, as it is seen by many people, must be given its dues, and recognized as providing the antidote, at least potentially, to its possible poisonous effects.

Among these poisonous effects are the polluting of the atmosphere by unregulated MNCs. Here again, however, the negative must be placed against the positive encouragement of global environmental groups that result from the MNCs' fostering of the communication revolution. As yet, the negative effects of the Bhopals and Exxon Valdeses badly outweigh the positive, but it can be argued that the global world which the MNCs are helping to construct, even if in unintended fashion, carries the seeds of better things to come.

Whatever power MNCs exercise, they cannot command armies (except, perhaps, in the shape of private security forces), they cannot levy taxes on a population, and they are unable to pass laws in a legislative body, as the state is able to do. Thus it is difficult to measure the MNCs power in the usual terms. To borrow a phrase from Joseph Nye, who speaks of the "soft power" of the USA, i.e., its spread of its culture and authority, which permeates society, perhaps we can speak of MNCs as exercising their rule through soft power.

Whatever effective dominion is exerted by MNCs is largely tied to their role in the process of globalization. The latter's persistence is itself tenuous, in the sense that a nuclear explosion by a terrorist organization (for example, acquiring the weapon on the black market and transporting it in the hold of a container ship) or a breakdown of the worldwide computer system engineered by hackers or hostile powers could cause much of globalization to come to a sudden stop. Thus, the rule of MNCs, such as it is, requires the failure of such efforts, as well as of anti-globalization sentiment, to derail the globalization effort that undergirds the corporate regime.

(3)

Putting aside doomsday scenarios (and excluding anti-globalization from this category), we must take the world as it is and return to the question: who currently rules that world? Let us approach this question now with MNCs in mind by taking a slightly different tack. I want to ask: is there a global elite in which the corporations are a/the core element? While there may not be a ruling class, as Marx and others had it, there can be little doubt that traditional economic and political elites have existed in the past, as depicted by various studies. In general, these elites have taken the form of national elites. With globalization transcending national sovereignty in many ways, is the emergence of a global elite a new addition?

On the assumption that such an elite is coming into existence, we need to ask who comprises it, and how they exercise their power and for what purposes. Is such an elite homogeneous, though we know it to be made up of different segments—such as business, media, military—and how do these segments relate to one another? Do the MNCs and their executives play a dominant role? In attempting to answer these questions, we must remember that, needless to say, the nation-state has not been disappearing, or even withering away, and we need to inquire into the ways national and then regional elites form part of a global elite.

A few comments can be hazarded. The first is that the existence of English as the new *lingua franca* enables members of the global elite to communicate with one another easily. Thus they inhabit roughly the same linguistic world. Next, and without question, this elite is overwhelmingly male. Females do exist in the global elite, but they do not play a major role, and certainly do not lead. Gradual change may be ahead, but even that is problematic.

One reason why change is possible, however, is that members of the global elite go to more or less the same schools. And today's business and legal schools are increasingly "manned" by women students. This potential, however, generally runs up against what is called the glass ceiling. Another choke point is in the meeting places of the elites, such as golf clubs and other supposedly recreational settings. The exclusion of women is not just a matter of rights but of power. A glance at the attendees of other venues of power, such as the Trilateral Commission or Davos, shows the same preponderance of men.

An Asian counterpart of Davos is BOAO Forum for Asia CEO Summit, whose meeting in 2005 was held in Hainan, PR China. Here, too, the attendees were almost all men. What is of further interest is how little over-lap between the members of Davos and of BOAO there seemed to be. A conscious effort was certainly made to keep the meeting Asian in focus, with the USA, for example, excluded. A quick glance at the invitees, however, suggests that the same sort of interests are represented at the Hainan meeting as at Davos, with equally impressive backgrounds in the corporate world. In both settings, the business and governmental world meet and exchange views as to how national and global policies are to be formulated and to go forward, both in their regional domains and more globally.

Whichever part of the world they live in, members of the global elite have similar lifestyles. There are even periodicals that tell them where to stay, what clothes to wear, what restaurants to patronize, and whom to know. Though as yet there is no manual of the CEO à la the manuals of the courtier of an earlier age, the equivalent is available. The result is a cosmopolitan leadership, easily recognizing one another in the corridors of power. Busi-nessmen, lawyers, accountants, management consultants all speak the same language and wear the same suits.

To make the global elite more concrete, a colleague, Elliott Morss, advanced the hypothesis that there is not one but four global elites. He argued that the first derives its status from social and family backgrounds; the second from its power to develop and implement profit-making ideas, e.g., Microsoft; the third from a top position in a state, e.g., president of France, or a global organization, such as the World Bank; and the fourth from its role as managers of global organizations.[6]

Yet there is no conspiracy among these members of the global elite to rule the world. The result, however, when we add in military leaders, is in fact a hand covered in velvet influencing and guiding our global society. It is not particularly a visible hand. This fact accords with the nature of globalization as a matter of flows and processes, where power is not located in fixed institutions, other than as they foster globalization itself. It is instead a kind of "virtual" power, growing naturally out of the information revolution of our time. Here, it would seem, we finally have an answer to our question of who rules the world.

(4)

I want to conclude by reiterating my argument that MNCs do not rule the world as such, or at least not by themselves. While they make up a large part of the global elite, they are not alone in its composition. Instead, MNCs are in a ceaseless though not inevitable competition and cooperation with other factors, creating the globalization that sets the conditions of rule. If I am right about our present-day version of the invisible hand, the problems of our time may not be so much located in the rulers of our world but in the fact that there is no "ruler" as such.

Even when MNC leaders are linked to military leaders—the famous military-industrial complex that President Eisenhower warned against—as well as the other sets of leaders mentioned, the result is not a world simply driven by them and the institutions they head. In an Age of Globalization it appears that a headless rider is in the saddle, with great power but little control. It is a scary thought, but one in accord with many of the facts to be found in the course of other work in New Global History.

Chapter 5

The NGOs movement

Nation-states, national forces, and, as we have seen in the previous chapter, MNCs are all leading actors on the international and global stage. Another increasingly important actor is the non-governmental organization (NGO) (under whose heading is also included international non-governmental organizations), an entity which is best treated as being part of a gathering social movement. Thus, one observer declares that: "The role of NGOs in the twenty-first century will be as significant as the role of the nation state in the twentieth."[1] Another speaks of a "global associational revolution," and refers to NGOs as a "fifth estate."[2] However hyperbolic such statements may be, there is little doubt that they point in a significant direction.

In Chapter 2 I gave NGOs a preliminary glance. Now I wish to put a spotlight on them at center stage. In doing so, I want to emphasize that we need to look upon them as both cause and effect of globalization. In their multitudinous forms, NGOs spread especially the juridical and cultural messages of the global perspective. Of equal importance, they step into the breach unoccupied by the nation-state and the MNCs in regard to governance structures. In taking on these tasks, the NGOs form what we can regard as a profound social movement. On the other side of the causal equation, NGOs have been arising like the proverbial mushrooms in the rain as a result of the actions, or inactions, of other actors in the globalization process; as I shall argue, they act frequently as the counterpart of the MNCs, as the handmaidens of ill-equipped nation-states, and as the carriers of racial, ethnic and economic minority hopes, not to mention the hopes of the whole of humanity.

Given their importance, potential and present, it is extraordinary how difficult it is to get a firm grip on NGOs, in terms of definition, numbers, range, type, etc. In the chapter on MNCs I mentioned the project that mapped them. That project was unusually successful in its immediate aims. As noted, both an historical atlas and a volume of essays resulted as planned. In producing them, an acceptable definition of what is meant by an MNC was easily arrived at, and, with much effort, the empirical data concerning the origin, spread, power, etc. of these new Leviathans were accumulated and visually represented. It is not clear as yet, however, to what extent the long-range aim, to change the way in which large numbers of people see the globalizing world, has been realized. That realization will depend on the spread of the idea.

A similar project, to map the NGOs, is encountering much greater initial difficulty. The definitional problem is horrendous, the data collection mind-boggling, the relation of NGOs to civil society daunting. All this in spite of an enormous collection of first-rate literature on the subject(s). The challenge is matched only by the need to meet it, for it is imperative today to see the globe, as with the MNC, in its true globalizing colors. In one sense, the present chapter might serve as a prolegomena to a possible mapping project, an example of how empirical research might be combined with theoretical speculations.

(1)

As with all other aspects of NGOs, their definition is much contested. Most observers would agree that they are not set up or run by states or governments, but arise as voluntary and not-for-profit organizations, hence NGOs.[3] At this point, contention arises over which organizations are to be included. Should those that promote commerce or are business oriented be put in this category? (My tendency is to do so.) Should churches and church-related institutions fit in? Ought we to distinguish, say, between the Catholic Church and Catholic Relief or Catholics for Free Choice (my own view is that the first does not belong among NGOs, and the latter two do). Simply to mention these few examples is to demonstrate the different opinions on the subject that can readily be found.

What further complicates the matter is that many of our potential cases are ambiguous. As George Thomas points out, many NGOs receive money from governments, and often administer substantial percentages of state aid monies. Lines are not firmly drawn between governments and NGOs; yet to exclude some of the latter on the grounds that they are therefore not really non-governmental is to miss seeing that states are "outsourcing" some of their work to these new organizations. So, too, it would mean ignoring the fact that the image of NGOs as pure, clean activist groups is just that, an image, and the reality is a messy one in which they become implicated with other actors in other sectors, and have mixed intentions and results.[4]

Even the question of what we are talking about is not simple. There is a spectrum of sorts running from IGOs (international governmental organizations), to INGOs, to NGOs, again with many crossovers. Terminology can vary: QUANGOs, or quasi non-governmental organizations, is a preferred non-American term for NGOs, thereby reflecting the ambiguities referred to above (see the OED, 1997 Additions). The question of tax status can be another crude measure. For example, in the USA one could assert that an

NGO is an organization that has 501 C status. For purposes such as ours, however, of seeking to understand NGOs in terms of a global perspective, this last definition appears to limit the inquiry rather than to further it. Again, I prefer a more inclusive definition.

As it happens, the first usage in English of the phrase NGO, according to the *OED*, is in 1946. As we know, of course, what have come to be called NGOs existed before the word. Again we face the Molière problem, as when the French playwright has his bourgeois character, enlightened by a tutor as to the difference between poetry and prose, declare in astonishment, "Oh, so I have been speaking prose all my life!" The lesson we bring from the play is that behavior may exist long before consciousness of that behavior. That consciousness, then, becomes as much a fact about NGOs as their first entrance on the stage of history.

Thus, though it is both important and essential to go back to earlier forms of NGOs—perhaps Islamic charities, anti-slavery movements, women suf- fragettes, and so forth—we must maintain the awareness that something different entered the post-WW II world. Extent, intensity, level of penetra- tion of society, and consciousness of the development, these are all constitu- ent of the NGO as a profound cause and consequence of globalization as it is presently developing. Most importantly, the NGO takes on new attributes, especially as it exists in a context of globalization (which itself is being newly understood).

To push this thought a bit further, an example emphasizing the word "organization" might help. Thus, nineteenth-century anti-slavery societies were organized in a manner very different from the way they would be today. Though slavery was seen as an international problem, pressure was largely brought upon legislators in a mainly (but not exclusively) national context. Literary texts were a prime means, the printing press a prime weapon. The anti-slavery movement (and one notes the word) was primarily a matter of elite opinion, influenced by a loose set of organizations. Contrast this with such a society today. It would be global in its reach, recruiting members and organizing them into a computer network. It would undoubt- edly seek to work in conjunction with the UN. Its ability to bring the matter before a global audience would be great. In short, it would be a global organization. And in this way it would be part of an overall NGO movement.

With all this said, we must also realize that the global NGO social move- ment has tended to be Western in its origins and to have a Western defini- tion. In the eyes of many it certainly pushes Western values and is probably a part of imperialism, overt or covert. Blatant in the nineteenth century in the case of the Salvation Army, it may take more subtle form in numerous twentieth-century NGOs, especially of the INGO variety.[5] So, too, many non-Westerners object to the individualistic assumptions of so many NGOs in contrast to their own societies' emphasis on communitarian impulses. In the eyes of some, Western and non-Western, NGOs are simply an expression of a bourgeois society and its values (we will see the same problem arise with the concept of civil society).

(2)

In mapping the MNCs, reported on in the previous chapter, the growth in their numbers from their beginnings in the 1600s, as expressed visually, took on the appearance of a J-shaped curve. These numbers were relatively easy to establish. The task is much more demanding in regard to NGOs. Hard numbers are incredibly difficult to come by. The compilation of the list of NGOs at particular points of time and in particular locales is a work in progress. Fortunately, for our purposes here, pending the further work of the mapping project, we need only recognize the general direction in the growth of NGOs.

If we restrict ourselves to INGOs, much easier to identify and count, we can see how they have proliferated. As John Boli and George Thomas, for example, tell us, "they have done so spectacularly, from about 200 active organizations in 1900 to about 800 in 1930, to over 2,000 in 1960, and nearly 4,000 in 1980."[6] The two authors reported this development in 1999, and clearly more data have accumulated since then. Operating, however, with the data available up to 1980, we can see that if we were to map them as we did earlier with the MNCs, a similar J-shaped curve would emerge. This should not surprise us, for, as we suggested earlier, the rise of NGOs and MNCs appears to be correlated, with the former being called forth by some of the actions of the latter.[7] Needless to say, the INGO curve starts later in time, and has fewer entries up to now than the MNCs.

INGOs are of many types: scientific, technical, professional, medical, and business-related ones account for the greatest number. They generally tend to operate below the radar of public notice except in special moments, and it is INGOs such as Amnesty International or Doctors without Borders that attract our attention. Yet globalization is fostered as much by the setting of technical standards and the establishing of communications infrastructure as by the moral/political activities of the better known INGOs. There is no need to derogate one at the expense of the other. They are engaged in the same social movement, along with the sports organizations that sprang up in pre-1991 Eastern Europe, all operating outside the formal state apparatuses and regimes.

Unfortunately, the figures I have been offering are Western in orientation. The Japan NGO Center for International Cooperation (JANIC), itself a non-profit networking NGO founded in 1987, offers a list of 116 Japanese NGOs whose activities are directed to overseas good causes. Here, too, we see how the conversation is bedeviled by the confused language of INGOs and NGOs. Comparable figures are needed from other areas of the globe, such as Latin America, the Middle East, and the whole of Asia.[8] The Caucasus has its own NGOs with overlaps to INGOs, as does Africa. In short, a comprehensive effort to map the number of NGOs, their growth curves (or declines if this were in fact the case), their range, their membership, etc. is vital if we are to look toward a fuller understanding of globalization in this sector.

(3)

Of all the INGOs, those devoted to human rights are central. As INGOs, of course, organizations such as Amnesty International and Human Rights Watch escape the tight hand of the state; being devoted to human rights, they also transcend the boundaries of tribal, ethnic, religious, and national affiliations. Thus, they epitomize the globalizing tendencies of our present world.[9]

Human rights is an historical construction, both as idea and partial reality. As idea, it is espoused by philosophers such as Immanuel Kant, and attached by affinity to the additional idea of cosmopolitanism. Paul Gordon Lauren prefers to treat the idea as a series of visions, whose inspiration and emerging reality he treats in his excellent book *The Evolution of International Human Rights*, showing how human rights were conceived and then achieved parturition in various parts of the world but particularly in the Western societies of the eighteenth century and thenceforward.[10] Coming to the end of his story, he offers a quote to the effect that "human rights became 'the single most magnetic political idea of the contemporary time'."

This is certainly a striking claim. In more mundane terms we may see that, as another author puts it, "After World War I, concern focused on guaranteeing rights by treaty for certain racial, religious and linguistic minorities in the defeated states. . . . World War II finally convinced states that human rights is a global issue."[11] Thus, we are confronted with the same sort of "history" that I sought to sketch earlier: one effort to expand rights, e.g., to slaves, leads to others of various kinds, until with the war of 1939–45 we find the effort extended to all humanity.

The midwife in this case is the UN and the NGOs attached to it. The story of the UN Declarations has already been touched on in Chapter 3. Here we need to remind ourselves that the UN may be thought of as a birth of Siamese twins, where one is attached to the fervent belief in national sovereignty and the other to a different "sovereign," peoples and their rights, not states. At the very beginning, in this context, to change metaphors, NGOs were a general force operating in society, spreading the notion of human rights, existing in the air so to speak. Very quickly, however, they were accorded formal consultative status. As William Korey informs us in one of the earliest and best accounts of the development, "A recent study offers the following data: only 41 NGOs held consultative status with the UN

Economic and Social Council in 1948; 20 years later, in 1968, the total reached nearly 500; 25 years later, by 1992, the figure surpassed 1000."[12]

Neither NGOs nor human rights had it all their own way. Quite the opposite. Fervid opposition was offered in the UN by countries afraid that the various Declarations and the attempts to carry them out would expose their own potential violations. Often willing to approve in principle, numerous states were quick to make sure that principle did not become practice, vitiating any attempts to set up effective enforcement mechanisms. Then at the UN's beginning and now, repressive states keenly recognized the UN/NGO connection and blocked or shut down the work of the latter in their home countries. Two of the most recent repressions and curtailments have occurred in Vladimir Putin's Russia and in monarchist Nepal.

Nevertheless, human rights and their practice were placed front and center on the global agenda. That agenda, however, is open to vigorous argument. The idea itself is attacked, in the name of local rights and traditions, say, by China or various Islamic countries. It is challenged as emphasizing individual over community rights, political above economic and social rights. Its universalistic premise is sharply questioned, and proponents of Asian values, in an inversion of the charge of Orientalism, appear to press for a part of the world to be seen as "inhuman."[13] (Of course, the retort is to claim that humanity is not all alike, but that this hardly adds up to inhumanity.)

Human rights, and the NGOs and other forces that fight for them, make many people anxious and defensive. In the French Revolution, rights were opposed to privileges. The same is true today. Different privileges—power, gender, and property, for example—come readily to mind, and few people like to give up privilege of any sort. An even more fundamental challenge embedded in human rights is its privileging of "humanity" as the constituency to be borne in mind when debating about such matters as climate control, nuclear regulations, the arms trade, and a host of other surging global problems. Such a constituency displaces the state, or religion or ethnicity, etc. as the reference for legislative and executive action. No wonder its adherents hail human rights in semi-religious terms and its opponents see in it the hand of the devil. In all of these fights, NGOs are at the forefront. They claim to be the self-appointed conscience of humanity.

(4)

It will not have escaped the reader that NGOs are involved in many fights on many fronts. Of primary significance is their role in regard to governance. Governance is not government—NGOs, after all, are non-governmental. Rather, as P. J. Simmons and Chantal de Jonge Oudratt remind us, the term governance "signifies a diverse range of cooperative problem-solving arrangements, state and nonstate, to manage collective affairs."[14] A vacuum, or no man's land, is created by the flows and processes of globalization, and into this space step NGOs when governments falter. For problems that transcend the usual geographical and institutional boundaries, new means of, so to speak, going with the flow have had to be devised.

Let me give one example, showing how state governments, the UN, and NGOs conspired to produce a judicial body, an international criminal court, in order to handle on a permanent basis crimes against humanity. Its origins, of course, lie in earlier attempts to handle charges of genocide: the failed Constantinople trials circa 1919 to deal with the murder of over one million Armenians by the Ottoman Turks in 1915 (a raging battle has reawakened over whether this is to be called genocide or a massacre); the more successful Nuremberg trials of WW II (not to mention the often overlooked trials of a similar nature for the Far East, to deal with Japan), where the term genocide was introduced along with the more general concept of crimes against humanity; and the subsequent international courts called into being to deal with the Yugoslav and Rwandan mass killings. At the end of this line is a permanent International Criminal Court (ICC), hardly a completely new idea, but marking a quantum jump of an "old" idea.

What is new is that it is a permanent international tribunal with global jurisdiction. Thus it forms part of an emerging global governance structure. The ICC took shape in a conference convened in Rome in 1998. Here 160 states, seventeen inter-governmental organizations, fourteen specialized agencies of the UN, and representatives of 250 accredited NGOs took part in the final drafting of the statute. The Rome meeting did not come out of nowhere. In 1994, for example, more than 800 NGOs formed a coalition for an ICC. Other NGOs advocated the new court in other venues. As one legal scholar sums it up, "The non-governmental groups mobilized political support and worked to advance the principles of accountability and redress for victims," victims who otherwise had no one to speak for them.[15]

The ICC was set up in the face of strong opposition from a number of countries. China, Russia, and the USA all viewed it as an infringement of their national sovereignty, and ultimately refused to sign the agreement, which nevertheless went into effect without them.[16] Here, I believe, we have a crucial test of the two parts of the UN—the one pointing in the direction of national sovereignty and the other to peoples' rights—and their ability to work together on a global scale. Adherence to the ICC serves as a kind of litmus test of intentions. Yet even without intention one can see a movement over more than half a century toward a global governance structure to deal with problems that can no longer be handled capably and alone on a local, i.e., national, level. It is hardly to be wondered at that those whose privileges are threatened by this drift of affairs are strongly opposed to what is happening—and to the NGOs that are playing so large a role in this development.

Opposition to NGOs can take place on other, more substantial grounds. In speaking of NGOs and governance we must not only take account of their effect externally, but also turn the question back on the NGOs. They claim to speak for those who have no other voice. But who has authorized them to do so? Nobody has elected them. What is the nature of governance within their own ranks? The issues of accountability and transparency arise as much with NGOs as with the MNCs. If NGOs are to participate in governing the world, on what basis can they claim to do so?

These are hardly unexamined issues. For example, a Global Accountability Project offers a guide to raising and dealing with such questions (see http://www.oneworldtrust.org). Periodicals such as the *Economist* periodically report on how, for example, NGOs that lobby an organization, such as the EU, use the very same money granted to them to lobby for further funds.[17] Frequently NGOs engaged in the same effort fight one another as much as their presumed targets, and so forth. In short, the reality of NGOs and their activities is often far removed from their shining ideals. For these carriers of governance, then, *Realpolitik* all too frequently trumps their vaunted moral purity. In this, they are all too like the states whose efforts they seek to supplement.

More intellectual challenges to the governance claims of NGOs come from other quarters. One scholar, for example, analyzes them in the same marketing terms as those used in the case of MNCs. His intent is to show that the "brand name" NGOs, such as Amnesty International, pick and choose the local NGOs they will support with a close eye on how it will play on the international stage. Will it increase their own visibility, their own ability to raise funds? Just as INGOs clamor for support from the UN and other agencies (including the public), so lesser NGOs clamor for support from the INGOs which alone can give them the visibility they so desperately need. Only if the given NGO can "market" itself in a way to make it stand out from all the other worthy NGOs does it have a real chance to succeed. In short, both INGOs and NGOs have what may be seen as a seedier side to their noble claims to be the conscience of humankind.[18]

In a more philosophical vein are attempts to examine the fundamental underpinnings of NGOs and what they stand for. I shall offer two instances to stand for many. One calls into question the belief that increased interdependence, along with a conviction about increased dialogue, will lead to more equity. The first author argues, instead, that asymmetry characterizes the dialogue, fostered and masked by the rhetoric of interdependence, as if all voices were equal, and thus does not lead to more justice.[19] Another argues that a speed-up of society—or what we might call increased time/space compression—at first enabled and supported democratization, but past a certain point a reverse effect occurs.[20] This second author does not make the application to NGOs, but we can certainly do so.

Seen from these lights, our "associational revolution," as embodied in NGOs, is a very complicated and debatable matter. They can be seen to be as much a problem in global governance as a solution. Even beyond, in regard to all the other functions they seek to perform, the same judgment might be made. This is not my view. Stumbling, fumbling, fudging, and nudging, NGOs as a social movement are a major, almost dominant factor in present-day globalization. As someone said of religion, if it didn't exist, we might have to invent it. NGOs in their expanded nature are as much an "invention" of the global epoch as the satellites and computer networks that make much of their work possible. That NGOs trail clouds of dark "glory" cannot obscure their contributions to our globalizing world. Only perfectionists would demand the unblemished ideal.

(5)

I do not wish to leave the topic of NGOs without placing them, finally, in the context in which they belong: civil society. NGOs are not the same as civil society, but they are a part of it, and we need at least to glimpse that whole. In antiquity, the idea of civil society was equivalent to the state or political society. This equation was broken in the seventeenth to eighteenth centuries in Western Europe, when civil society arose in opposition to the absolutist state. We must pause and note that the development of the nation-state turns out to have been requisite for the emergence of the modern civil society. At this time civil society at first meant the realm of economics, whose "free" markets stood separate from though protected by the state. Toward the end of the century of Enlightenment, it came to mean public opinion, a counter-weight to the secrets of raison d'état. In this realm, marked institutionally by the salons, the cafes, the Masonic lodges, and the academies of the time, the critical, rational spirit was presumed free to roam without restrictions other than civility.

Briefly, then, this is the heritage of civil society.[21] As a concern it seems to have faded in the second half of the nineteenth century. It takes on new life in the second half of the next century. Then the context was not the absolutist state but totalitarianism, specifically that of the Soviet Union. Thus in Eastern Europe the only form in which opposition could effectively take shape was in terms of voluntary associations (many of them sporting ones). Solidarity in Poland, or Vaclav Havel's dissident group Charter 77, are more impressive examples. Their success made civil society a hot subject, linked closely to the likelihood of liberal democracy.

Before going further, a few attempts at abstract rather than historical definition. It is useful to follow up on the historical origins of the concept, noting that civil society is "a political space, or arena, where voluntary associations seek to shape the rules that govern one or the other aspect of social life."[22] Another try, somewhat more abstract, informs us that it "is the sum of institutions, organizations and individuals located between the family, the state and the market in which people associate voluntarily to advance common interests."[23] An even more philosophical approach, taken by Jürgen Habermas, tells us that "civil society is made up of more or less spontaneously created associations, organizations and movements that find, take up, condense and amplify the resonance of social problems in private life, and pass it on to the political realm or public sphere."[24]

As can be seen, all emphasize the manner in which civil society stands in regard to state power—a kind of unspoken challenge to national sovereignty—while necessarily cooperating and working alongside that power. While most definitions and discussions seek to align civil society associations with liberal democracy, this is by no means a necessary connection. Such associations flourished under absolute monarchy in the seventeenth century, in fact were called forth by its existence. In the late twentieth century, although such associations may have aimed at some form of democracy, the fact is that they existed for a decade or more in Eastern Europe under a non-democratic system.

If this fact is accepted, then one can seek to extend the conceptual reach of civil society into non-Western societies. Thus, scholars examine the possibility of its existence in the Muslim world, for example, in terms of taking particular Islamic forms, such as the *waqf*, or charitable trusts (the counterpart of foundations in the Western world), or seek to show how Islamic traditions can co-exist with this aspect of modernity. Defining civil society as a mélange of associations, clubs, guilds, etc. coming together to provide a buffer between state and citizen, some Islamic scholars argue for its co-existence with their religion and particular state systems.[25] The same consideration can be found in Chinese studies, which in general are pessimistic about the space available for civil society in Chinese traditions and the present-day Chinese communist state system.[26]

What holds our interest in these discussions is the place available for NGOs in the globalizing world. As I am suggesting, NGOs are a part of, not a proxy for, civil society. Thus, at the same time as we are told of the difficulties of establishing civil society in the Arab world, we noted that there the number of NGOs grew from about 20,000 in the mid-1960s to over 70,000 late in the 1980s. They are one means of expressing the civility and the aspiration for participation in the governing process that can be found in all sorts of societies. When these organizations link in various ways with other NGOs and INGOs around the world, they become part of a social movement.

As such, they join with other forces that are working toward a new form of civil society: global civil society. We are talking about an attempted whole, in which international criminal courts, innumerable agencies of the UN (directed at problems, for example, of the environment, nuclear regulation, security, diasporas, and refugee population movements), and a host of other institutional efforts to deal with issues that transcend traditional boundaries are in dialogue or conflict with national sovereignty. In focusing on NGOs, I am seeking to view them in the context of this larger whole, a new global civil society. By their very definition, NGOs allow us to think beyond the existing bounds of nationhood, ethnicity, religion, while sometimes fostering their aims, and permit us to imagine and work toward other, larger bonds.

(6)

Fostered by the gaps in governance created by globalization, and facilitated by the computer revolution, NGOs of all kinds, dealing with a whole host of issues, large and small, move in a momentous social movement. Sometimes in conjunction with government bodies, sometimes in opposition to them, they have become an indispensable part of the globalization process. Able to escape or circumvent the control of communications by states, standing in an often awkward aloofness from existing political parties (though, as the Greens show, sometimes being aligned with them), they need to be approached as both an ideal animating humanity and a reality that is "human-all-too-human".

Part III

Policy and morality

Chapter 6

The hijacking of global society

Globalization, I have been asserting, is by now a generally acknowledged fact. Its outcome, the nature or kind of global society that is being created, however, is a matter of conjecture and contestation. There are a number of different versions on offer, and I want to identify and discuss three leading ones. These leading contenders are: 1) a global civic society, 2) an Islamic global society, and 3) an American, or Americanized, global society. In what follows I continue to make the assumption, already argued in other chapters, that the process of globalization itself is neither teleological nor deterministic, but rather contingent in its development upon many factors. A fortiori, the same is true for global society.

(1)

A leading player in the attempt to study global society is the *Yearbook on Global Civil Society*. It offers as a working definition: "the sphere of ideas, values, organizations, networks, and individuals located primarily outside the institutional complexes of family, market, and state, and beyond the confines of national societies, polities, and economies."[1] Crucial to emerging global society is the information revolution, with its computer network allowing for the transcendence of national and local boundaries. Obviously, if states can block or censor the exchange that takes place on the net (as a number do), the movement toward a global society is slowed down if not thwarted.

In the *Yearbook*'s version of that movement, a key term is "Civil." As Martin Shaw in the 2003 *Yearbook* tells us, "Civil society itself is a pre-global concept that is now being transposed into global terms."[2] I have already treated civil society in relation to NGOs in the previous chapter. It is important to repeat here that in its "pre-global" form, for example, in the eighteenth century, civil society was composed of economic actors, i.e., market organizations, as well as civic associations. Both were seen as counterweights to the state and to the family, operating in something that came to be called the public sphere. Only in its global form, today, is the economic actor sometimes displaced from civil society. In my view, such displacement is questionable.[3] MNCs are certainly separate from the nation-state, transcending its boundaries, helping to create civil society, and operating in its general sphere. Though at present most MNCs behave in a rogue fashion, they may not always do so in the future, and they compose, in principle, part of the "public sphere." The move to increased corporate social responsibility programs points in this direction.

The temptation to exclude economic actors arises from the definition of the public sphere as one of sociability, in the service of the greater good. Yet in the eighteenth century, there was much debate about the market economy as a source of virtue and the promotion of democratic values, as well as cosmopolitanism. That potential still exists, though obscured by the current neo-liberal version of economics that for the moment dominates as the ideology of the MNCs: the pursuit of profit to the exclusion of all other goals. This inclination also obscures the fact that the MNCs are one of the leading engines in erecting the infrastructure undergirding the construction of global society and its "civic" nature.

We recapture the essence of that earlier debate when we remind ourselves that the process of globalization and its resultant society should be seen as a civilizing process elevating humankind from a national and regional level to a global one. The elimination of violence is one part of that civilizing process, and this elimination or at least reduction may require the transcending of national sovereignty. Another goal, having often to use the same means, is justice. When these goals, and similar ones, are pursued in the name of an abstraction, Humanity, the constituency is global. In this regard, a cosmopolitan gaze (in spite of the criticisms noted against it in the previous chapter) is *de rigueur*.[4] Of course, what is being described is more an ideal or direction at the moment than a reality. Still, the appearance worldwide of 11 million demonstrators against the Iraqi War suggests that part of the ideal is becoming reality.

One author, Mary Kaldor, claims that a fundamental change in regard to sovereignty took place in the 1990s.[5] Subsequent events suggest that we may be witnessing a two steps forward, one step backward movement. In any case, what is evident is that globalization is leading more and more to the emergence of some sort of global society. What actual shape and form such a society will take are the subject of debates, which have the effect of both analyzing the present and influencing the future. Let me confess that my sympathies lie in this direction. Others, however, are antipathetic to the global society and the direction in which it might carry us. As Kaldor and her colleagues recognize, in regard to global society there are rejectionists, as well as supporters, along with reformers.[6] I am suggesting that in addition to these three camps there are those who simply have alternate ideas of a desired global society.

(2)

One such alternative is that of Global Islam. It is a vision that sees Islam spreading to all of humanity. With this simple statement, however, we enter an enormously complicated and many-layered topic. From its very beginnings in the seventh century, Islam in principle knew no borders. Like its comparable monotheistic religion, Christianity, the religion preached by Mohammed was for all peoples, anywhere on earth. Starting in the city of Mecca, in the Arabian peninsula, it spread rapidly until by the twelfth century it was in control of a huge empire, with its center in what we have come to call the Middle East, stretching from the Mediterranean to the lands of Asia. A principal enemy over time was Christianity, which had a comparable global message and mission. Prototypic of the conflict were the Christian crusades and the Muslim conquest of Spanish lands.

As a glance at the long history of Islam shows, the reality was that, in spite of its claims to a global reach, Islam (like Christianity) was limited by geography and political strife to only one part of the world (indeed, much of the actual world was still unknown, e.g., the New World continent; the first physical globe as such, in fact, was not constructed until 1492, by Martin Behain).[7] Our task, however, does not require us to enter into that history in detail, but only to be aware of it as background for our engagement with Global Islam today, as a contending vision of the global society produced by the present-day phase of globalization.

In undertaking this study, it is probably well to be aware of the distinction made, for example, by the scholar Mehdi Mozaffari, who defines Islamic as a term referring to a "religion and culture in existence over a millennium," and Islamism as "an Islamic militant, anti-democratic movement, bearing a holistic vision of Islam whose final aim is the restoration of the caliphate."[8] Nevertheless, bearing in mind this distinction, I will mostly use the more generally accepted phrase "Global Islam" in what follows. In doing so, it must be made clear that Islam itself has many mansions, and most of them are not occupied by what have come to be called fundamentalists and even more narrowly terrorists.

In any case, we are dealing with a vision of Islam that transcends all borders. From its beginnings, as we have noted, Islam claimed to be universal. Our concern is with the effort today to realize that vision in practice, in a world that is becoming increasingly globalized. Let us note that the radical version of Islamism dominating the news today makes no distinction between religion and politics, a position within Islam not generally accepted and the source of much contention (as, for example, in Iran). Let us also note that ambivalence characterizes much of what is at issue: the desire for the global spread and dominance of Islam co-exists with an intense desire to protect existing religious/ethnic divisions within traditional borders.

My focus is on the radical transcending vision, a vision that seeks to make the ideal actual by a partial embrace of globalization even in its Western form, or at least to capture some of its results. To even partially understand what is happening, we must go back a bit in time. First aware at the end of the seventeenth century, with the failure of the Ottoman Turks to take Vienna, that the balance of power was shifting, the Muslim world was shocked into fuller awareness with Napoleon's intrusion into Egypt at the end of the next century. Faced with the onslaught of Modernity, as were so many other parts of the non-Western world, the Muslim/Arab world sought to come to terms with it in many ways during the nineteenth and twentieth centuries.

In other words, before globalization there was modernity. From the beginning there were attempts to imitate the European version. Thus, Mohammed Ali sought to "modernize" Egypt in the 1830s. His effort was undercut by the French and the British. Many other such blockages by the forces of imperialism litter the pages of the history of the area. A major part of European modernity was nationalism. It inspired Arab intellectuals and leaders, including Gamal Abdel Nasser in the second half of the twentieth century, but was cramped if not crushed by the imperialist powers. The same can be said of the nation-state. Artificially created out of the dismembered Ottoman empire, national entities such as Transjordan and Iraq struggled to become other than failed enterprises. Even when successful, such nation-states as Saudi Arabia were undemocratic, often corrupt, and held together by tribal and religious bonds rather than secular ones.

The failure to cope adequately with modernity often fueled a sense of inferiority and humiliation. This latter is a key word in regard to Global Islam. One finds it repeatedly in the writings of the Ayatollah Khomeini; and more recently it appears twice in the short fatwa of February 23, 1998 of Osama Bin Laden.[9] A glance at any day's news from the Middle East shows the obsessive use of the term humiliation. Admittedly, a sense of humiliation is not absent in either personal or political life elsewhere. I suspect that its extreme power and omnipresent usage in the Middle East come from the region's dedication to honor and dignity, rooted as these are in the tribal loyalties of so much of the population.[10]

In any case, that sense of humiliation and failure in the face of modernity is compounded by the coming of modernity's new face, globalization.[11] Falling behind even further, Islamic societies have floundered in their reaction to the globalizing forces. One result of these forces is a reinforcement of the sense of local and particularistic identities. Why this is a surprise to some social scientists is itself a matter of surprise: that to every action there is a reaction should hardly come as a novelty. What may be, in fact, really surprising is that the local in this case tends to share a widespread desire for an imagined united past. In that past, the caliphate was superior to the West, and Islam was pure and uncomplicated. Pure and uncomplicated, of course, are exactly what modernity and globalization are not.

At the other end of the spectrum from the local is presumably the universal. There is no contradiction, however, in this case, as we saw from our earlier consideration of the origins of Islam. Building upon the local beliefs, and seizing upon the very instruments of globalization—the overcoming of time and space, the use of immediate communication devices everywhere, the weaponry of high tech, e.g., missiles, the propaganda reaching across the world, etc.—radical Islam declares itself a global movement whose aim is the conquest of the world. As the saying goes, if you can't beat them, join them—and thus beat them.

Employing the techniques more usually characteristic of MNCs, Global Islam has sought to organize itself as a worldwide unified entity. Thus, Al-Qaeda, which means "The Base," from 1997–8 on brought together previously disparate groups devoted to terror and opposition to the West. Al-Jihad, whose roots were in the struggle in Egypt, headed by Bin Laden's second-in-command, Ayman Al-Zawahiri, was one such group; mujahidin trained in the war in Afghanistan was another. Alliances were made with Palestinians (whose desire for their own land was mainly local), Moroccans, Tunisians, Indonesians, and so forth, sometimes in tenuous ties and sometimes in more lasting ones. The result was, and is, a military force—terror— with global reach, and inspired by a vision of conquering the globe in the name of Islam.

Its adherents have waged a war without borders. In the words of one summary, "they have devastated embassies in Kenya and Tanzania, blown a hole through the USS Cole, and flown airplanes loaded with passengers into the World Trade towers and the Pentagon; they have bombed synagogues in Tunisia and Turkey, mosques in Baghdad and Karbala, a night club in Bali, apartment complexes and military barracks in Saudi Arabia, and three days before a national election in Spain, commuter trains in Madrid."[12] Less explosively, but more extensively, they have brought fear and consternation to much of the globe, disrupting and challenging ordinary daily life. The war without borders has, in effect, invaded the "Homeland" of the most militarily powerful country of the modern, globalized world.

There is little need to go into more detail. By now it should be clear that one alternative to Global Civil Society is Global Islam. The latter is aided by an increase in population in the Middle East due to the availability of advanced medicine and the high fertility of the region encouraged by Islamic exhortation. This population pressure, in turn, leads to increased migration, fostered by all the elements of globalization (such as easy transportation, communication, job needs, etc.), with Muslims in Europe, for example, increasing by leaps and bounds. Such migrants are often made unwelcome in their host countries, especially by far right groups arising as a natural reaction to the perceived "invasion," resulting in yet another turn of the humiliation screw for those of the Islamic faith. The latest newspaper stories now tell of radical Islamic preachers, for example in Great Britain, telling their young followers to court martyrdom in destroying their godless hosts.[13] Thus Global Islam takes on the image of the enemy within as well as without.

How serious is this contender? In my opinion, Global Islam simply does not have either geography or politics behind it, anymore than it did in the past. Terror, in this case in the form of radical Islam, is the weapon of those who are weak in military and political terms. This is not to say that it cannot disrupt the societies it attacks, now on a global basis. Nor that in a convoluted fashion it may not drastically affect, even derail, the process of globalization leading to a Global Civil Society. Contingency is a word that must always be in the historian's mind. It is merely to say that the society being created by globalization will not be one dominated by Islam, though any such society must certainly come to terms, as part of its commitment to humanity, with Islam as a part of its own civic nature.

(3)

The other major contender, and more successful one, in defining the shape of the global society resulting from globalization is the USA. It has been the most supportive of economic globalization through the mechanism of the free market. To some observers, neo-liberal economics is a means of achieving not only economic domination but political power as well. As one scholar puts it, "the process of globalization has been driven most crucially by the enormous political power placed in the hands of the American state and of US business through the particular type of international monetary system and associated international financial regime that was constructed— largely by the US government—in the ashes of the Bretton Woods system." Consciously or unconsciously, institutions such as the IMF and the World Bank were constructed so as "to entrench the United States as the power that will control the major economic and political outcomes across the globe in the twenty-first century."[14] This has been the policy, more or less, of all administrations, certainly from Nixon onward. It is, therefore, an *American* policy, not merely that of a particular administration, such as that of George W. Bush. His contribution has only been to make the policy more obvious and egregious.

To fully grasp this point, we must reenter upon a historiographical argument concerning the nature of globalization. In the eyes of economists and economic historians, as we have noted, economics is almost synonymous with the globalization process; all else is window dressing. To other students of the subject, other aspects, such as the political, the cultural, the social, the technological, are intrinsic parts of the phenomenon, and only separated out by disciplinary scissors. In reality, of course, globalization is holistic, and the economic is as much political and cultural, for example, as it is a purely "economic" matter. If this framework is accepted, we can then choose to emphasize a piece of the action, in this case the political.[15] In doing so, we can focus on the international system of sovereign states as the mechanism through which the US asserts its hegemony and combines both its free-market and nationalistic inclinations in its drive to dominate global society.

This fact has been obscured by another fact, that in the decades up through the 1970s the US appeared to foster the transcendence of national sovereignties. It participated, for example, in the Nuremberg trials, was instrumental in the creation of the UN, and supported the Declaration of Rights. Meanwhile the American espousal of the free market meant that multinational corporations, for example, were aided in their remaking of the world by the forces of global production and consumerism. Another result was the accidental spreading of American culture, at the same time as making that culture itself more global in content and nature. All of this, of course, was in the context of the gathering Cold War, in which American power projections meant large numbers of troops in Germany and Japan, and subsequently South Korea, inter alia.

Appearances were deceptive. US support for the non-military developments was predicated not on the belief in the building of a global society but on the conviction that such global-directed institutions in fact served American national interests and would remain under American control. If not, they were to be opposed. The roots of this belief lie deep in America's history and persist, as already suggested, through particular changes in administrations. It is easy to forget that it took almost two decades for the US to sign the First Geneva Convention (in 1882). Thus, the late twentieth-century opposition to international agreements, whether in regard to the Criminal Court, the Land Mines Treaty, the Kyoto Accord, or a long list of similar initiatives, should come as no surprise. While the Bush administration is more strident and undiplomatic in its opposition than previous administrations, its positions are in tune with the American tendency to protect its own national sovereignty when that is seen as threatened.

Today, this is obvious. Thus when the *National Security Strategy* 2002 document, for example, speaks of "today's globalized world," and of "an increasingly interconnected world," it does so not because it actually accepts such a world but because of the awakening blast of September 11.[16] In response to the latter, the Bush administration sets forth its own version of a "globalizing mission": the creation of what some call an American Empire. This American mission stands in opposition to the movement toward a global civil society that gathered force in the half century or so since WW II, in so many different forms and so many different countries. In this light, the new empire can be seen as a so far successful "hijacking" of globalization, in the same vein as the global terrorism it fights.

(4)

Let me try to give content to this assertion. The key is national sovereignty. The forces of globalization are, by definition, transcending it. The constituency for global society lies in international organizations and in NGOs that seek to operate in the name of humanity, increasingly becoming interconnected in actuality through such agencies as the World Wide Web and other manifestations of the information revolution. The paradox is that the USA, which has been and still is so instrumental in the creation of global society, is unwilling to live as a citizen in the world it has been creating.[17] Repudiating its offspring (other parents, of course, such as Japan exist), America is attempting to press the forces of globalization into a Procrustean bed that fits only the American frame. Extolling its own national sovereignty, the US takes as its global mission to make the twenty-first century an American one and to convert or force others to adopt its own image of democracy and capitalism.

The rhetoric is not mere hypocrisy. Those who mouth the words of democracy and international cooperation sincerely believe in them. The problem is that they are engaged in self-deception, for there is a disconnection between what is said and what is done. The giveaway, for example, is in the proclamation of the *National Security Strategy* of 2002, announcing that: "The U.S. national security strategy will be based on a distinctly American internationalism that reflects the union of our values and our national interests."[18] Translation: endowed with a heritage of exceptionalism, we will do what we wish, as the only superpower, resorting to international cover whenever possible. The corollary to this position is the elaboration of the doctrine of preemptive and preventive military action.

National interest is joined, of course, to the shibboleths of national sovereignty and national security. For example, Rwanda was declared not to be part of America's "national interest"; thus the USA had no commitment to doing anything about its spate of genocidal war. The same recently was the case with Liberia and its terrible killings—so much for the gesture toward internationalism. As for the Balkan involvement, according to one account: "The [Joint] Chiefs never believed that Kosovo, by itself, was vital to the U.S. national interest."[19] As is well known, the USA simply stumbled into the war against Milosevic. In the case of Iraq, that troubled conflict, it was entered into in opposition to much of the international, let alone global, community and justified initially by charges (subsequently unproven) as to Saddam Hussein's possession of nuclear and chemical materials intended for use against the USA and his alleged (false) backing of Al-Qaeda. Surrounding all its actions has been the assertion of American national sovereignty and security, which could only be maintained by unilateral action with whatever allies could be gathered around it.

The contrast with the needs and aspirations of a global society is apparent.

In a global society, other peoples' lives are as precious as our own. When asked how he felt about the prospect of 200,000 Iraqi dead as the result of the US invasion, the president's senior advisor and political campaign 'guru' Karl Rove replied: "I am more concerned about the 3,000 Americans who died on September 11."[20] Neither Christian nor global in value orientation, such a callous and cold-blooded assertion resonated with a selfishness preached in other areas of American life. It was in tune with the business ethics displayed by many firms (though certainly not all) and taught in most economic classes and business schools across the country. It reflects a unity of vision and value pervading the international and the national area, with the two being conflated.

Further insight into American attitudes is given by some most interesting survey data. It shows the American public as being smug about its innate right to rule and highly nationalistic in its general views. Indeed, it is a kind of hypernationalism, or superpatriotism, so full of itself "that it cannot easily be contained by geographic borders," with Americans "so convinced that their nation is a force for good in the world that they have difficulty casting a critical eye upon U.S. global policy." As the author of the survey concludes, "A strong, perhaps overdeveloped, identification with nation underlies the pervasive belief that the U.S. must don the mantle of world leadership—using military power, if necessary, as its own trump card. In fact, given the choice between thinking of themselves as American citizens or as citizens of the world, few Americans even give the latter a passing glance."[21]

The mindset described above shapes the American response to an increasingly globalizing world. It is one shared by leaders and led, more or less equally. Of course, such nationalistic egoism is not unique to the US. What is unique is that the US is in a position, militarily, economically and politically, to act on its belief, and in the process shape the emerging global society in its image. That image, when realized, is different from the one held by proponents of global civil society.

Needless to say, there are many extenuating circumstances for American actions today. Global terrorism is a real threat. The UN and other international agencies have been weak and hesitant in both intention and action. A secure and effective global institutional order is barely discernible, and the Bush administration might charitably be viewed not so much as pursuing foreign policy unilateralism as desperately trying to fill a void. Indeed, in the eyes of many of its supporters, the US is not so much asserting its own national sovereignty as hemorrhaging from the surrender of its national sovereignty to global bureaucrats.

Whatever truth there is in some of these statements, the bottom line is that the US does not see its own future in terms of a truly effective global civil society. The result is that it has set its course for the next American century, in which the world is made secure in its image and not by common

agreement and consent. Marching to a different drummer than its traditional European partners, America has helped create a breakdown of trust
and a conflict of goals that threatens the future direction of global society.
One major result is the loss of the moment of promise in the 1990s and a
setback that may last decades for those who believe in the possibility of
a more equal and just globalized world.

(5)

"What ifs" are viewed by historians with curled lips. Yet they serve as a
useful comparison to what has happened, illuminating the latter and its
consequences more fully. What if the US had seized the opportunity of the
last decade to act as the leader in moving to a more just global society? What
if, instead of exacerbating its long-time dislike and scorn for the UN, the US
used its vast power to support the organization and its efforts to bring peace
and justice to the world? What if the US threw its support behind the
International Criminal Court, the Land Mines Treaty, the Kyoto Accord and
so many other attempts to deal with global problems in a global manner?

While clearly such actions would not miraculously bring about a perfect
world, they would appear obviously to move us in the direction of a better
world. Instead of the pie in the sky, i.e., national missile defense, decided
upon unilaterally, a concerted move toward control of nuclear materials
could have been pushed. Instead of a pinched-off effort in Afghanistan,
a truly concerted effort—and here the US had willing allies, such as
Germany—could have been made to rebuild the country after the defeat of
the Taliban and put it securely on the path to its own version of self-
government and a sustainable economy. So, too, the Israeli–Palestinian
stalemate, the mutating cancer of the Middle East, could have been dealt
with by a coalition of European and Arab countries led by the US in a
forceful manner and with a firm voice. Here, if anywhere, an enforced solution, not entirely satisfactory to either side but "fair" in the circumstances,
could have been evidence of global purpose.

What about Iraq? The overthrow of Saddam was certainly a breach of
national sovereignty that could potentially have been justified, as was Kosovo, in the name of humanity and human rights. In many ways a laudable
global project, it was turned into its opposite: the unilateral assertion of one
nation's rights of national sovereignty in the name of its national security
interests. If the decision had been made by a UN–US led coalition in the
name of humanity and as one of a number of possible similar decisions to
come when circumstances permitted, the prospects of global society would
have been advanced. There is no shame in acknowledging that Iraq was
invaded "because it was possible," unlike the situation in North Korea. The
shame is that it was done for no better reason than that the US wanted it,
and had the military power to do it.

These what ifs illustrate the road not taken. Instead, a president who first preached that withdrawal from nation-building was the correct response to globalization jumped to the other extreme after 9/11 and proclaimed a crusade to make all the world America. In place of what I am calling global society, and its slow and hesitant efforts to shape a just response to our present-day globalizing circumstances, a projection of America and its power was put forward. What is called the American Empire, of course, presumably can be thought of as one response to the globalizing forces around us. As I have presented it, to repeat, it is a hijacking.

It comes at a moment of tremendous opportunity to move forward to a more democratic, diverse, more moral global society, often promoted as a civil society. That opportunity is being squandered, or, more sharply put, perverted by the American notion of a "global" society. It is a moment that may be gone for ever, or, if one is optimistic, merely for a number of years, when momentum toward it can be resumed. Only future history and historians will be able to tell us what happened. At this moment, however, we seem to be in the midst of a tragedy.

(6)

A global society of some sort there will be. I have suggested the three major forms it may take. The contenders are Global Civil Society, Global Islam, and Global America. The middle term, Global Islam, does not seem a likely winner, no matter its short-term successes (which certainly does not mean that Islam itself will not be a powerful shaping force in whatever global society emerges further along). While we have not been accustomed to think in these terms, and it is a dismal and dismaying prospect, the real fight will be between the first and last terms. As with Global Islam, that fight must first be waged within Global America, bringing its citizens into the global society they have been helping to create. Events and education in the broadest sense will help shape the outcome of that struggle. The process of globalization, as remarked upon earlier, is a contingent, not a deterministic one.

Chapter 7

The global and the local

At the core of present-day globalization is the *problematique* of the global and the local. Amidst the debate that emerges on this subject there is generally much passion and less thoughtful analysis. The problem itself, of course, is hardly new, only the form in which it confronts us. The "local" can be the family, the tribe, the state (as in states' rights in the USA) and the nation, each in contest with the other and all potentially now against the global. With the global entailing a major time/space compression, it is hardly surprising that the "local" requires a new "location" in our thinking, as well as in our everyday life.

The problem itself is deeply rooted in the origins of classical sociology, illustrating once again how global studies must operate in an interdisciplinary fashion. There we find the attempt to analyze the nature of social bonds sitting at the center of inquiry. Implicit in this attempt is the concern with the global and the local, though not expressed in these explicit terms. When Ferdinand Tönnies, for example, writes of *Gemeinschaft* and *Gesellschaft*, he is intuiting the later arguments on our subject. The same is true of his compatriot Georg Simmel when he speaks of the difference between the mentality of the small town and the metropolis. The French sociologist Émile Durkheim posits the issue in terms of a society based on division of labor and one grounded in religious forms of life. The greatest of the German sociologists, Max Weber, places his emphasis, of course, on the market, which he tells us is "a relationship which transcends the boundaries of neighborhood, kinship, group, or tribe," and obviously has powerful effects on what it creates and what it has transcended.[1]

By the second half of the twentieth century the terms of discourse have shifted and the dichotomy global/local emerged. This is now one of the major new ways in which the concept of social bonds is discussed. Present-day sociologists such as Roland Robertson, John Urry, and Sylvia Walby, to name just a few, are carrying on the older tradition. They are doing so in the light of present-day globalization, whose transcendence of established boundaries has been foreshadowed in the passage quoted above from Max

Weber. The connection of the past debates and the present ones obviously presses itself upon us.

It is also true that this debate has been carried on in regard to other, related subjects: cosmopolitanism, civilization, modernity, these other frigates of thought on which we try to navigate the currents of social existence, also raise the issue of the near and the far, the particular and the universal, the us and the them. Cosmopolitanism especially bears on the topic, and will need to be brought into the present discussion as we seek to situate our loyalties. Though we glance further at it, our main focus will be on what the sociologist Roland Robertson has provocatively labeled "glocalization," the way in which the global and the local intertwine.[2]

That "way" can be manifold, for there is no single set of relations. What can be said of the United States of America, for example, may not be said, say, of Japan. The global may be more or less the same in both countries, but the relation to it of the local varies greatly. This poses a challenge for us. In this chapter I make general statements having mostly the American example in mind. I do so in the belief that my preference for the global and even the national over the local as a source of the moral holds true even while I recognize that there are qualifications that may be required in regard to various situations. For example, "public" in Japan is equated with bureaucrats, who place self-interest and narrow views over the general good. Thus, there is a strong movement in that country to decentralize government power and strengthen local autonomy, in the belief that the local will better represent the good of the people.[3]

In this case, we are told, the local expresses itself through NPOs (non-profit organizations), for the local legislators, like their national counterparts, often malfunction. As of 1996, there were around 86,000 of these NPOs. Spurred into existence by the Great Hanshin-Awaji Earthquake in 1995, and the inadequate response on the national level, as well as by an ageing population whose needs were ignored at the same level, resort was had to NPOs as an expression of local autonomy. Thus, it would seem, the local is the site of the higher morality.

Without going into further details, I merely enter two caveats to this conclusion. The first is that such higher morality is not found in the local governing bodies, which are little better in this respect than the national bodies. It is based, rather, on NPOs; and these are the offspring of the global imperative. As one scholar puts it, "the trend toward globalization . . . is a critical factor in Japan's decentralization process." As he goes on, "while globalization exposes the smaller regions of the world to the global marketplace, its values may take precedence over local values, so that, when a country's political, economic, and developmental activities become globalized, the national government may cease to be dominant."[4]

If I read this author correctly, it is globalization that opens the way to the better localism of the NPOs, by weakening the competence and reach of the nation-state. In short, what starts out looking like a contradiction to the thesis that I advance in the rest of this chapter ends up being simply a qualification of its details. Other, comprehensive studies would be useful to see if the same result would hold, but that is not the task I undertake here. Rather, having flagged some of the complications that adhere to the subject, I turn now to the exposition of the thesis I wish to advance concerning the values to be attached to the global and the local.

My inquiry is into two parts of the problem. Why, I ask, is one or the other, the global or the local, preferable? Why not, in fact, accept that each carries its virtues and vices within itself? In this part of our inquiry, I argue that there is a myth of the virtuous local that causes us to overlook its attendant evils. Thus, an unbalanced picture results. In the next part of my inquiry, I try to look at some of the "facts," i.e., the actual manifestations of the local and the global, in their conjunctions.

(1)

A good starting definition, already quoted in part earlier, of the globalization of which we speak is offered by Sylvia Walby, describing it as "a process of increased density and frequency of international or global social interactions relative to local or national ones." Here the global/local issue, presented in terms of "social interactions," is made the heart of the definition. Yet Walby wishes to disclaim the notion of "Supraterritoriality" to be found in so many other definitions of globalization, for she insists that "global processes still have a territorial component." Fleshing out her definition, Walby identifies its causes as "the increased power of global capital markets; the rise of new information and communication technologies; and the rise of a new hegemon which creates the conditions for increased trade."[5]

A definition such as Walby's has the virtue of being equally germane to the particular problem of the global and the local. It allows us entrance to our subject by a recognizable portal: a door opening on a theory of social inter-action. It connects us to a large literature that takes as its object the way people construct social bonds. The idea of social bonds, mentioned earlier as the core of the discipline of sociology, really only comes forth, consciously, in the West in the seventeenth century, when the concept of society emerges. It is followed in the next century by nationalism and the nation-state, the revival of discussions about cosmopolitanism, and the reification of the notion of civilized into the abstract noun civilization, all in the face of an impending democratic and industrial revolution that threatens to break all connections between man and man (not to mention God and Nature). One further result, of course, is the "birth" of "sociology" as a discipline.[6]

There is one more piece of apparatus I wish to erect before turning fully to our subject. It is the structure of thought that emphasizes expression of the global and the local in terms of the universal and the particular. Where eighteenth-century cosmopolitans grasped the universal as their particular form of identity, early romantics identified themselves in terms of the particular itself. It is, they argue, the non-generalizable, the non-calculable, the non-repeatable that characterizes life as against the sterile expressions of the universal and the mechanical. The sound of the battle, for example, is heard in the comments by Georg Forster, the Swiss/German anthropologist, who had accompanied Captain Cook on his voyages in the South Seas, and who wrote a fragment on Indian poetry called "On local and universal culture" (1791). Taking a firm stand, Forster wrote that: "The local, the specific, the peculiar must melt into the universal, if the prejudices of partiality are to be vanquished. Universality has taken the place of the particular European character, and . . . [the latter] can be styled as the representative of the entire species."[7] To the romantics, of course, such a view was anathema.

Change the words a bit, and we are engaged today in the battle of the global and the local. In place of the romantics, we can put postmodernists. Many of them, too, extol the particular, emphasize the relativity of things, and distrust the universal and the global. They stand opposed to a meta-narrative that claims to tell a story of progress, of modernization, in which globalization is merely the latest version of modernization. For postmodernists of this persuasion, there is virtue only in the local and the particular, as they are seen to refuse to give way before the sharp razor of reason and rationalization.

In one sense, *plus ça change, plus ça reste*. In the battle of the global and the local there is for the historian a feeling of déjà vu. Yet, to take this view would be to ignore what is new in this contest, and to neglect to give attention to the particulars that characterize the present-day process (or processes) of globalization. The past gives us a comparative vantage point, a historical context, in which to place our latest developments. It cannot substitute, however, for a fresh inquiry into the "happenings" of our own time.

(2)

My impression is that, aside from a small group of ardent globalizers, the weight of general opinion is on the side of the local. Admirers of the local can find support in the words of de Tocqueville, who wrote that: "The strength of free people resides in the local community. Local institutions are to liberty what primary schools are to science; they put it within the people's reach."[8] In addition to being the bedrock of liberty, the local is seen as warm and reassuring, a home whose embrace protects one from the blasts of an outside and threatening world. It can take the form of communitarianism, along with the other forms ranging from the family to the nation listed earlier. It can embrace the "habits of the heart" as contrasted with the putative cold, sterile claims of the rational and universal. It can stand for roots in an era of broken ties and loyalties. In the terms of postmodern architecture, it can extol "place" as against abstract space.

I would like to concede all of these attributes and then argue that the local is also heavily freighted with the parochial and the limited. It is hardly news that the local is often self-centered in its concerns and hostile to needs outside itself. It also represents entrenched power, which defends its particular interests in the name of locality. It misrepresents its own interests as well, by focusing on the short rather than the long-term effects of its own actions. In so doing, it has an adverse effect in the longer run on other localities.

How do we balance the virtues and vices of the local? Before attempting this summation, we need to acquire much more knowledge about some of its actual manifestations. In the (re)counting that follows, I shall highlight the actual workings of the local versus the global in terms mainly of its negative features, while not forgetting the positive.

It is a cliché that all politics are local. Implicit in this formulation is that particularist interests triumph over more general ones. Let us look at some examples of what is at play. An obviously heinous one is the decision by a tribal council in a Pakistani village that a young woman be raped in revenge for a crime allegedly committed by her brother. Such "local" decisions are generally overlooked by the government. Should they be, or must a trans-local standard of justice be brought to bear on the case, representing a wider interest of society than that involved in the tribal council's decision?

This example and countless others like it are blatant and tendentious. It is obvious (except to fanatical relativists) that in such cases a higher locality must step in to counter the narrowness of the particular local. Let us jump now to a much higher locality, in this case the nation, and in this example the USA. A few years ago, local steel industry leaders and unionists prevailed on the Bush administration to undercut its own free-trade policies, favoring globalization, in the name of political calculation. Local politics—for the Bush people needed the votes of the constituents in these critical rust belt states—won out over the interests of the general American consumer as well as the administration's general commitment to the global.

Perhaps this was a good thing, and the promotion of the global in this case a false goal? Can the same thing be said of the case of Pakistan, where the country was originally rewarded for its posture vis-à-vis the September 11 event by a waiving of duties and quotas on textiles and clothing, a waiver that was then rescinded under pressure from American lawmakers from textile states? In a world where all politics are conceived of as being local, the woes of Pakistani workers are as nothing when set again the interests of a small minority of Americans, a case of the local triumphing not only over the global but the national. A similar story can be told about US trade with Chile and with countless other countries.

Perhaps I can dramatize the conflict by taking up the case of slavery and civil rights in the US. Enshrined in the Constitution and defended in the name of states' rights, slavery was held to be sacrosanct and protected from outside interference. Only the Civil War in the middle of the nineteenth century breached the sovereignty of the slave-owning states and bent them to a "higher" law, that of the larger nation. Was it justified? Many in the former Confederate states say no and still cling to states' rights, with their particular state claiming precedence in some cases not only over the United States but over even more local sovereignties within the state in question.[9]

As is well known, even in defeat after 1865 local resistance to equality for blacks persisted in highly successful form in many of the Southern states. The civil war had to be renewed in the twentieth century in the form of a civil rights movement. Sheltering behind the door of states' rights, Arkansas, for example, refused to accept Federally mandated requirements to end educational segregation. Only the sending of Federal troops and marshals ended the stand-off and imposed national standards over the local ones. Again, local sovereignty was invaded in the name of a higher morality and law.

In short, as the examples so far given show, the local must often give way to a larger "local." The national has its rights that the lesser locality knows not. The local cannot simply be a talisman to wave off all possible intervention by other forces. In thinking about the global and the local, perhaps the former must be thought of as simply the larger "local" above the national one. If this is so, the former Yugoslavia and its recent history may replace the former Southern states as our example, with no sovereign right to abuse its own people in violation of their "human" rights. In fact, it is a situation such as the Yugoslav, and comparable ones, that insistently demand that we get right the equation between the global and the local.

(3)

Until the coming of the global, i.e., present-day globalization, the local found its antithesis in cosmopolitanism. Does this offer a source of identity that effectively transcends the local? Is it itself a result of local conditions? Does it offer the possibility of a belief system that can inform and improve the way the parochial and the political limit the possibilities for the general good? Or is cosmopolitanism a will-o'-the-wisp, floating too high above actual, local life to give effective guidance of any sort? To glimpse answers to such questions we need to say more about cosmopolitanism itself.

Its origins, as we well know, are in Greek antiquity. Its hero is Diogenes, who, in addition to looking for an honest man, dismissed the Greek polis as the source of meaning for himself and others, and in its place declared himself a citizen of the cosmos. Thus, the local is swept away as a place of attachment and identity. In its place is the world as a whole. Diogenes, the famous Cynic, was then followed by the Stoics, culminating a few centuries later in Marcus Aurelius. Emperor of the Roman Empire though he was, he declared that "my nature is rational and civic, my city and country . . . is

Rome." But then he concluded, "as a man, the world." In this hierarchy of identifications, it is the latter that is highest and the local that is of lesser importance.

With the decline and fall of the Roman Empire, cosmopolitanism faded away, submerged in the rival ecumenism of Christianity, whose City was significantly not of this earth. Even more crushingly, cosmopolitanism disappeared in the feudal Middle Ages, where particular fealties reigned supreme. Emerging fitfully in the intervening centuries, it is not until the eighteenth that cosmopolitanism reassumes an important role in the discourse of philosophy and social existence.

A good starting point for our understanding of eighteenth-century cosmopolitanism is the short entry in the *Encyclopédie*, "Cosmopolitain, ou COSMOPOLITE, (Gram. & Philosoph)." Reading it, we are told that the cosmopolite is "un homme qui n'a point de demeure fixé," or rather "un homme qui n'est étranger nulle part." The term's etymological roots in the Greek are given, and then its origin in antiquity is underlined by a last sentence, wherein we are told that an ancient philosopher, asked whence he came, answered, "Je suis Cosmopolite, c'est à dire citoyen de l'univers." To which the writer of the entry adds, "Je préfére . . . ma famille à moi, ma patrie à ma famille, & le genre humain à ma patrie."

These brief allusions to the "history" of cosmopolitanism can allow us to draw a few conclusions. The first is that it emerges from local conditions and can serve local purposes. In the case of Diogenes he is seeking refuge from the political pressures and iniquities of the polis by appealing to a community outside and beyond it: humankind. (Christianity will do the same a few centuries later, but in religious rather than secular garb.) With the *philosophes* of the Enlightenment, cosmopolitanism becomes a belief system by which to measure the shortcomings of absolute monarchy. By claiming the only citizenship available to them, in the cosmos, the *philosophes* implicitly are laying claim to a more local citizenship as well. In this vein, cosmopolitanism can be viewed as an ideology, and one of its outcomes, though it is mainly a contributing cause, the French Revolution.

Cosmopolitanism is also an aspiration. This is our second conclusion, and it points to the inspirational nature of the cosmopolitan vision. Rising above its local, ideological purposes, it offers a conviction that places the social bonds of humanity at large above those of family, city, and state. Implicitly, it asks: why and how am I more connected to my immediate neighbors than to others at a greater distance? By the time of the Enlightenment, the social bonds in actuality were greatly extended, by trade, by technical innovations and improvements in communication, and by a more tightly knit international system of states. The political implications of these developments were only partially recognized. The *philosophes* who embraced cosmopolitanism were ahead of their time, intuitively aware of the direction in which events were carrying humanity.[10]

That direction has been toward globalization. Not deterministic, not fated, globalization has been developing out of systemic forces within the modern world. Economics has been a powerful propellant. The quotation from a debate on the Napoleonic Code of Commerce given earlier highlights the direction in which humanity was headed. As a proponent of one clause in the Code exclaimed, "The bill of exchange has been invented. In the history of commerce this is an event almost comparable to the discovery of the compass and of America ... It has set free movable capital, has facilitated its movements, and has created an immense volume of credit. From that moment on, there have been no limits to the expansion of commerce other than that of the globe itself."[11] In the words of this little known debater, long before Karl Marx made the expansion of the world market central to our understanding, the shadow of globalization stretches before us.

Of course, as insisted upon throughout this book, an immense number of other factors than the purely economic (there is, in fact, no such thing) were to be involved in this development. Nor is it an unimpeded development, of simply linear dimensions, one without interruptions or set-backs. Nevertheless, a general line of march can be detected in the history of the past few centuries. It is as part of this march that we must also note that cosmopolitanism as an intellectual commitment had faded and more or less disappeared as an ideology in the nineteenth century in the face of nationalism and internationalism.

What about cosmopolitanism today, in a global epoch? It is startling to observe how a number of authors have attempted, so to speak, to capture cosmopolitanism for the local, i.e., to localize its universal reach. A number of quotations will make this clear. The anthropologist Arjun Appadurai, for example, argues for a "cosmopolitan ethnography" in his book *Modernity at Large*, whose subtitle is *Cultural Dimensions of Globalization*. By this he means the study of "lived experience in a globalized, deterritorialized world"; or, as he explains further, "Today's cosmopolitanisms [note the plural] combine experience of various media with various forms of experience—cinema, video, restaurants, spectator sports, and tourism, to name just a few—that have different national and transnational genealogies." Such an ethnography, he adds, can lead us "to an understanding of the globalization of Hinduism, the transformation of 'natives' into cosmopolites of their own sort."[12]

A literary critic, Bruce Robbins, distinguishes a new cosmopolitanism from the old "abstract, ahistorical universalism," and proffers a somewhat convoluted redefinition: "As a practice of comparison, a range of tolerances and secularisms, an international competence or mode of citizenship that is the monopoly of no one class or civilization, it [cosmopolitanism] answers the charge of 'particularism' and 'loss of standards' ... because it presents multiculturalism as both a common program and a critical program."[13]

(Where Robbins speaks of secularisms, of course, Appadurai has made room for religions such as Hinduism.) In any event, another anthropologist, Paul Rabinow, tells us that "critical cosmopolitanism" is a good thing. "Let us define cosmopolitanism," he suggests, "as an ethos of macro-interdependencies, with an acute consciousness (often forced upon people) of the inescapabilities and particularities of places, characters, historical trajectories, and fates. . . . We are all cosmopolitans."[14]

One last quotation, this from Lila Abu-Lughod and her attempt to prac-tice Appadurai's "cosmopolitan ethnography" in the field, specifically in an Upper Egyptian village. What she finds is that the concept of cosmo-politanism is applicable to those who stay at home as well as to "those who travel, those who feel at home in several parts of the world." The vehicle is television, which, though its "meanings are produced some-where—for most viewers somewhere else . . . [is] consumed locally in a variety of localities." Thus, as one of her subtitles informs us, different versions of cosmopolitanism "confound the concept of 'cultures'," here identified with the local.[15]

These quotations are representative of the effort to blur the boundaries between cosmopolitanism, with its putative universal aspirations, and the local (sometimes referred to as cultural) embrace of particularism and place. Postmodernists, especially, have found this prospect appealing, as have exponents of multiculturalism. This position, even while "privileging" the local, has the virtue of acknowledging that peoples are now linked together in a global culture—perhaps better called global civilization—at whose core is multiculturalism. Thus, globalization, cosmopolitanism, and the local are all conflated.

Such a reconciliation would seem to accord with the fact that the cosmos has taken on actuality; that is, that all peoples, more or less, are now living as "citizens" of a common globe. What was ideal and utopian, e.g., cosmo-politanism in the Enlightenment, is now practical and potentially situated in real, or at least virtual, space. We begin to acknowledge this fact when we talk about the "global commons" and even about the misguided notion of a "global village." In this formulation, we are all becoming cosmopolitan tourists on the Internet, traveling in common in cyberspace.

Standing back, however, from this happy ecumenical prospect, we can raise a few questions. What happens when the local cultural knowledge conflicts with the cosmopolitan, universalizing knowledge, i.e., with global-ization, say, in the form of human rights? Similarly, it's all very well to speak of the "citizen" in the new global world; in fact, however, what are the rights and duties attached to that role today, and how are they to be enforced? There is also the issue: if all voices are to be heard, do they arrive with equal power? To raise such questions, and many more could be added, is simply to illustrate once again the complicated nature of the relation of the global and the local. In this regard, cosmopolitanism has become a stand-in for both sides, reconciling them but at the price of sweeping many of the difficult problems under the rug.

(4)

One school of thought can finesse these problems by simply making the case that we are dealing with an artificial division: the fact is that globalization, like nationalization before it, is actually local. A few examples should suffice to establish this position. The first is in regard to the nation. It emerges from scholarly research into the connection of the local and the nation, particularly in regard to nineteenth-century Germany. The thesis is that "localist or 'Heimat' sentiment is a constitutive and necessary feature of the nation-building process." Thus this view repudiates "the notion that the local was rendered obsolete by the national in the same way as the global then rendered the national obsolete."[16]

Instead, the local is seen as constituting the national at the same time as it threatens to undo it. As Alon Confino and Ajay Skaria argue, "the nationalist imaginary deploys the trope of the local to articulate the specificity of the nation; of how the local comes to be refigured as home—as the nationalist home."[17] Fleshing this out, another scholar tries to show how particularist patriotism—in the form of sponsoring museums, festivals, and the like—came to be seen as "variations of the whole, not as an alternative to it."[18] Such a view is in line with Edmund Burke's famous boast that "to be attached to the subdivision, to love the little platoon we belong to in society, is the first principle (the germ as it were) of public affections."[19] As with de Tocqueville, support is given to the notion that such small attachments are the basis, rather than the enemy, of larger ones.

Alongside these assertions by historians and political theorists can be found those of anthropologists. Here, too, the presumed opposition of the local and the global is dissolved. Thus, one fear on the part of the "locals"— that globalization means homogenization—turns out to be false upon close examination. In the case of the Egyptian villagers studied, as noted earlier, by the anthropologist Abu-Lughod, they have been preserving their own culture in the face of global cosmopolitanism flooding over them through their TVs. In fact, as she shows, the TV channels are owned by a multitude of different country-based companies, and their offerings are tailored to local consumption. As yet another account informs us, "The top TV show in South Africa is 'Generations,' a home-grown multiracial soap; in France, it is 'Julie Lescaut,' a French police series; in Brazil it is 'O Clone,' a telenovela made by TV Globo." In the words of one TV head, "The more the world becomes global, the more people want their own culture." Or, as the head of Walt Disney Television International puts it, "Viewers are essentially local in what they consume."[20]

On another front, what could be more global than the World Cup in soccer (which, unlike the so-called World Series in the US, actually has competitors from all over the world)? Yet, as one reporter tells us, "No single international event is experienced more locally than the World Cup—from the hometown bars to the soccer lots to the mood in the Presidential TV parlor. The results of a match can leave a nation reeling in self-doubt or swimming in a national euphoria." Then follows detailed accounts of "how it all felt back home" in Germany, Turkey, Poland, and other localities.[21]

In short, to sum up what has been said about cosmopolitanism and about the fact that globalization actually seems to be local, one conclusion might be that all of our problems on the subject have disappeared. The local is generally benign, and no different from the global. Thus, we can go back to praising the virtuous local and worry no further about its possible myth-like qualities. Is this, in fact, the case? I take the position that it is not.

(5)

My argument proceeds as follows. The first thing is to acknowledge that there is much to be said against the effects of present-day globalization. When it is equated with the free market, some of the results can be disastrous. Rather than improving the condition of the poor, it can be said to widen the gap between rich and poor without much improving the lot of the latter. What there is of global governance takes the form of the IMF, the World Bank, and the WTO, all under the thumb of the developed nations, and especially the USA. Their aim is all too often not the well-being of mankind, and their effects tend to be the economic and political dominance of the power holders.

While each of the assertions just made can invoke vigorous denials, the overall record is clearly a mix of good and bad, virtues and vices. The global is no different in this regard than the local, whose balance sheet was cast up earlier. Why then do I believe that it is important for us to discard the myth of the local? The answer is in the moral realm. Let me admit that there is nothing sacrosanct in larger social bonds per se. On all levels—family, tribal, regional, national, and now global—there is always a balance of the good and evil. Yet, having said this, we must go on to explore why the global is more likely than the local to serve the cause of humanity.

To make this case, we must return to cosmopolitanism. What was merely an ideal and an ideology in the eighteenth century in Europe has become, I have argued, an actual condition for many today. Whether we like it or not, we are linked in ever closer social bonds by the filaments of the Internet and by the messages and images bouncing off the satellites. My "neighbor" is just as likely to be an e-mail correspondent a continent away as the person living next door to me in my apartment building, whom I never meet. Without trivializing the importance of face-to-face interactions, we must recognize that our interests and identities have become more and more a matter of larger levels than the traditional "local."

Why does such a cosmopolitan condition entail the betterment of humankind? We get a suggestive response by going back to our example of the United States and its experience with slavery and the civil rights movement. In this example, from a moral standpoint the high ground was not to be found in the local, where entrenched interests prevailed. Only outside forces, benefiting less from the existing arrangements, could bring to bear a trans-state perspective that saw slavery as the evil it is—and do something about it. This entire problem involves a complicated argument, into which others are invited to enter. There needs to be a dialogue as to why the larger network of social bonds is more likely to be on the side of the angels than the smaller ones. My proposition is that as society approximates more closely to an identification with humanity as a whole—the cosmopolitan vision—the more likely it is to act in a manner consistent with that vision.

Today, the cosmopolitan vision is entwined with the global. It is crucial that, for example, corporate executives recognize the imperative of serving the well-being of humanity as much as that of their more local shareholders. Statesmen and women have to recognize the global world in which they are living and take it into account in their decisions, not bowing down automatically to the presumed exigencies of local politics. Intellectuals ought no longer to play their "local" games as if the world was not becoming global. All of these actors must take on a cosmopolitan character.

Needless to say, none of this will occur overnight, nor in the sweeping terms I have outlined. None the less, these changes can be facilitated if we look more closely at the overall problem of the global and the local. As I have observed, we must initially note the ways in which there is a false dichotomy at work here. Especially, we must be skeptical in regard to the myth of the local as the source of goodness. Overall, in a global epoch, we need further work, both empirical and theoretical, to help us in understanding the nature of the process of globalization in which we are involved, and especially the way in which the global may hold within it the potential for a "higher" moral sentiment.

(6)

There are two other examples, or aspects, of the global/local relation that need consideration. The first relates to the environment. The second takes up the way the global and the local produce results that then cycle back on one another.

What can be more global than the environment? Seen from space, the earth is a connected system. Its cloud cover is not just for one part but for the whole sphere. Winds on one part of the globe affect ocean currents in another. Satellites can now show us pictures illustrating how desertification and deforestation are spreading everywhere, and how carbon emissions affect the atmosphere, with consequences for ozone holes, global warming, and related phenomena. Consequently, we now see, not just think, the global.

Yet the environment movement in the US, for example, was first driven in the 1960s by mostly local, domestic issues. In various accounts, these are listed as local air and water pollution, strip-mining, highway construction, noise pollution, dams and stream channelization, clear-cutting of forests, hazardous waste dumps, nuclear power plants, exposures to toxic chemicals, oil spills, suburban sprawl. In this grab bag, clearly some issues are particularly local—Love Canal would be one example—while others quickly can spread to the more global—for example, the nuclear and toxic spill-overs.

Nevertheless, the environment loomed as mostly a local problem in the period before the 1970s, with the US being a leader in the movement to deal with it. The notion of an Earth Day originated in that country. As the decade unfolded, however, and as it became clearer that many of the environmental problems transcended national boundaries, international, i.e., global, efforts expanded, and the US retreated from the larger scene. The tipping point may well have been the 1972 UN Conference on the Human Environment, held in Stockholm. Whereas air pollution and waste disposal might still be adequately addressed at the local level, such other threats as fishery depletion, the spread of organic pollutants, and climate change required coordinated action around the globe and at the hands of new global institutions and jurisdictions. Challenges such as those taking the form of the "tragedy of the commons" (while it is rational for one fisherman to take as large a catch as he can, everyone doing it produces disaster for fishermen in general) or of public goods (who pays for clean air and an intact ozone layer?), with their attendant free loaders, simply go beyond local solutions.

In problem areas such as those sketched above, it does little good to invoke the mantra of the local. Of course, where possible, one solves a local distress with local means. The local here can mean either the neighborhood, the region, or the national. What needs an act of imagination is to realize that the local in many situations today actually means the global. We need to hark back to the definition of globalization as "a process of increased density and frequency of . . . social interactions." Such social interaction may be greater with a global "neighbor" across the seas than with the one who owns the adjacent lot to mine. Because the chains of connection with the former are lengthier in space and longer in time, and/or more abstract, they are harder to envision than those connecting me to the person next door.[22] They are, however, at least as important, and possibly more so. We, and especially legislators and leaders, must, it appears, raise our level of understanding to the level of actual global developments.

My second example can be presented in even shorter form. What could be more domestic at first glance than the politics in, say, France? How, then, can we see the hand of globalization in the far-right party of Jean-Marie Le Pen? A moment's reflection suggests the answer. Immigration, whether in France or all the other European countries, is intimately tied to the local issues of a stagnant economy, high unemployment, and the welfare system. Local voters are concerned with living standards, crime, and foreigners. Immigrants are seen as the cause of the decline in all the indices related to the subjects listed above. Immigrants come from other parts of the globe. The syllogism is complete.

The immigrants are the local result of the global, for, clearly, they are to a large extent a product of national decisions about tariffs, import quotas, etc. that ill-favor the development of the "native" and "local" country from which the immigrants come. If one throws in the policies of international institutions, the picture darkens further. What I am trying to suggest with these broad, bold strokes is how the local affects the global, and the global the local, and back and forth in a constant, almost Escher-like dynamic. The reality is "glocalization," of a most complicated sort. But our knowledge and comprehension, or way of looking at the world, is often excruciatingly local. That vision, or lack of it, enters prominently into what we have identified as a global/local dynamic, making it difficult to deal with problems that are already difficult enough no matter on what level we tackle them.

What I have been offering here are merely hints, initial probes, as to how one might try to impose some sort of system on the overall question being asked. The question has been from the outset: why is the one or the other, the global or the local, preferable? What is now needed is both further theoretical reflection and empirical case studies, limited "local" inquiries, which can then return us to our theories in a more informed fashion. This is the challenge to social scientists and philosophers alike, as we all face what has become a fundamental query of our times.

Chapter 8

Toward a higher morality

Globalization, as I have tried to demonstrate, is generally discussed in terms of the expansion of free markets, or of the spread of democracy, or the increasing hegemony of American-style media, i.e., in economic, political, and cultural terms. Much computer ink is injected into these topics, a copious literature exists on them and on related subjects. Needless to say, much debate still surrounds the role they play in globalization. The latter itself is hotly debated as to its definition. Such debates and discussions are all extremely worthwhile. What is given less attention is the subject of morality.

As one effort to remedy this situation, I have been raising the question: does increased globalization, in general, make for a higher level of morality than would prevail if local mores were left pristine? In the previous chapter, I argued that it does, and tried to show by specific historical references—e.g., to slavery and civil rights in the USA—that this is so, using a national transcendence of the local as my example. Now, I want to inquire more deeply into the reasons why increased globalization holds out the promise of greater morality, or what I am calling a higher level. Why, I am asking, is global opinion likely to be more moral than local?

In an age of relativism, multiculturalism, social constructionism, and post-postmodernism, to talk of a "higher" morality may appear absurd, if not incendiary. The notion, starting from romanticism and historicism in the nineteenth century, that peoples and cultures are incommensurable has warred constantly with the assertions of universalism. This notion has enjoyed a growing ascendancy in the second half of the twentieth century, and now on into the present century. Today, or so it is asserted, it seems almost self-evident that the idea of a higher morality, along with other notions of progress, has been swept into the dustbin of history.

It is useful to try to unpack this assertion. Along with Herder, it is Hegel who most vigorously advanced the idea of historicism. As he remarked in his *Philosophy of History*, "Every age has such peculiar circumstances, such individual conditions that it must be interpreted, and can only be interpreted by reference to itself."[1] A moment's reflection, however, reminds us that Hegel, nevertheless, also believed in progress—for him the increasing realization of Reason as humans become conscious of reason in history—along with the existence of a higher morality brought about by dialectical means in the human past.

Hegel's paradox, embracing both historicism and progress, has been swept away in the relativism of our time. Our present-day relativism is grounded not in history and historicism—the view that each age is peculiar to itself—but in anthropology and culture, and the view that each people or even segment of a people is peculiar to itself and to be judged only in its own terms. It is this latter "tradition" that, spurning the notion of progress, tends to validate the local as superior to the global and rejects the idea that there may be a higher morality embodied in the globalization process taking place around us. The very word "higher" is seen as an affront by many, as smacking of elitism, as well as simply being misconceived. Higher classes, higher values, higher culture, higher morality—they all run counter to the belief in principled equality and the leveling spirit prevalent in our culture.

It is essential, however, that we detach the possibility of higher morality from that of class, and deal with it in its own terms. Most people will have no trouble with this conclusion. We must do the same in regard to race or ethnicity. Here, however, we must start from the assumption that there are no higher and lower races or ethnicities. In fact, it is exactly the universalism embodied in globalization that allows us to make this claim and with it the claim that there is a higher morality that tends to transcend the local differences. As one result, in place of class or race or ethnicity (though these may have residual social reality), in globalization our major conceptual actor now becomes Humanity. Here we have the measuring rod held aloft by the great monotheistic religions in their better moments, as well as by philosophers ranging from the Greeks to the *philosophes*. Yet, it is only now that the ideal of humanity is beginning to take actual form in today's global interconnectedness and interdependence.

(1)

If the statements I have been making are accepted, then we can at least have earned the right to take up the topic anew. We can explore the reasons why globalization may carry a higher morality within its processes, defining what is meant by higher morality as we proceed. Our line of argument will run as follows. First, I will reemphasize the tightening of social bonds that marks present-day globalization, i.e., the reality of increased human connection that underlies the sense of humanity. Next, I will examine the role of science, i.e., knowledge, along with sentiment as the glue holding global society together. This will lead to an exploration of the idea of humanity as a social construct. It will also serve as the context for a renewed discussion of rights. Lastly, I will attempt to think about the way culture relates to morality.

Globalization, I have argued, is best looked at in terms of social relations.

Humans live together in many different ways, ranging from the family, small or large, to clans, tribes, nations, states, and numerous other groupings that can take the form of religious or ethnic communities. This cliché is the staple matter of much sociological investigation and theory. Present-day globalization has increased the social links between peoples who otherwise only experience one or more of the social bonds just listed. Their lives are marked by the greater density and frequency of social interaction, whether in terms of trade or culture, played out in a world where space and time have been extraordinarily compressed beyond anything previously known.

As a result, a growing number of social exchanges take place simultaneously as well as instantaneously. Large numbers of people are in touch with one another to a greater degree than hitherto. They can be mobilized across the globe. This is the global village aspect of globalization. It stands next to the more recognized intensity of economic exchange, the expansion of multinational corporations, and the ceaseless dynamic extension of capitalism. These phenomena, in turn, are connected to ever-moving science and technology (though the causal arrow will run back and forth). In turn, all of these are linked to global consumerism, of both material and cultural products. I need hardly go on in this liturgical strain as to the manifestations of present-day globalization.

The liturgy does establish, however, the *fact* of greater human social interconnectedness, necessary to my argument that follows. What do we make of it in regard to moral consequences? In a pioneering article, as I noted in the previous chapter, Thomas Haskell tried to show that the British bourgeois of the nineteenth century were awakened to the moral abuses of slavery by an extended communications net that did not allow them to pretend lack of knowledge of what was happening. Specifically, appeals to their humanity were made real by the evidence brought before their eyes. In the same way, the links that provided awareness also provided the means to do something about the problems made visible. Increased knowledge, coupled to increased sensibility, made for a greater sense of common humanity and the need to act in those terms.[2]

I want to expand Haskell's argument. Immediate visual awareness of horrors in the Congo or Afghanistan has an impact that makes the victims our neighbors, part of our common humanity, unless we block this awareness by an ideology of racial or nationalistic difference. The possibility of being immediately aware is present, in a way that it has never been before, for us to identify with these "others," now seen as part of ourselves, i.e., fellow human beings. Thus, globalization carries within itself the possibility of our having an increased moral responsibility for our counterparts anywhere in the world. They are with us in our immediate lives.

With this point established philosophically, I want to flesh it out historically. The example I choose is the national one. When a people come to feel as one, members of a common territorial state who are citizens, they are prepared to relinquish local interests and "rights" in the name of a broader community: the nation-state. Thus, it is accepted that a national legal system prevails over local laws and mores. Particular economic interests are to be overridden by those of the whole, as determined by a national political system, which speaks in the name of the economic interests of the body politic. In area after area, social, military, and even pedagogical, the same transcendence is supposed to prevail, in principle.

The reality, as we know, is often different. So, too, that reality, flawed as it is, has come about by a long historical process. The emergence of the nation-state, for example, is an "event" of the last few centuries, coming into being fitfully and differentially in particular areas. With the absolutist nation-state as background, we witness the rise of "society," the development of capitalism, and the shift from subjects to citizens. The struggles are many and, though de Tocqueville considered democracy a providential necessity, its rise has been episodic and fraught with constant challenges. The very territorial basis of such a state/society has been shifting and shaky, in spite of the assertion of inviolable sovereignty in an international system.

Many stories have been told about the rise of the nation-state and about particular examples within this rise. Most such accounts operate on the nation-state level itself, and are frequently recited about non-Western as well as Western societies. I want, instead, to recount only one small and even parochial part of that story, and thus to witness at close hand the move from a local to a national level. I will attempt to do so by using a work on New York City, *The Monied Metropolis*, by Sven Beckert. This may seem a strange choice, but I make it because it illustrates in such immediate detail some of what I want to say about nation-building, which I can then use in regard to discussing globalization.

In Beckert's account, antebellum New York was dominated by a commercial elite, whose power stemmed from the cotton trade and its connection to the plantation South. A growing manufacturing elite still stood in the shadow of this commercial interest. The horizon of this elite was the city, and only faintly in the background the new nation. It was the Civil War that shattered the existing urban hegemony. Backed by the Northern manufacturers, the war eroded the power of both the New York commercial class and the Southern land and slave owners, and strengthened the Federal government and its claim to override "local" interests in the name of the nation.[3]

Here in the proverbial nutshell we have a detailed and specific account of how one country, the US, moved from a largely provincial to a national level. Once at that level, the nation could move outward in an imperial reach, culminating at the end of the century in the acquisition of the Philippines. In this manner, the US became a full-fledged nation-state, with colonies, and could set itself up as the equivalent of its European exemplars. This entire development can be seen as a further empowerment of the

national over the local, and at the same time as a prefiguring of a globalization to come. Remaining at the national level, however, this development
offers us a vivid example of how citizens now had a state/society with which
they identified themselves and their interests. In the name of this national
identity, they were prepared to submerge particular and local claims (though
in practice, of course, fighting every inch of the way).

Will something similar take place in regard to global identity? That is a
question to be decided by the struggles of our time and those to come. On
the national level, peoples are required to be concerned about their fellow
citizens. Oppressive working conditions are to be regulated, if not done
away with, across the nation. Education and opportunity are similarly supposed to be available for all (no matter that in practice inequalities remain).
The aim is to approximate equal rights, even if asymptotically. Let us compare our emerging global society: will we be concerned with working conditions, say, in China, that make it possible for peoples elsewhere to have
cheap silk shirts without being disturbed that they may be depressing and
oppressing a fellow human being? (Of course, the same narrative may
be constructed about Chinese working in New York City in sweatshop
conditions. The difference in the latter case is that it is against the law.)

Whether global society and rights are arising or will arise is an empirical
question, whose answer I believe, on the basis of accumulating evidence, to
be in the affirmative. On the assumption that this process is, in fact, taking
place, I want to explore further the moral dimensions involved. The philosophical ought never to be detached from the historical, but it can be looked
at separately against the background of the latter. To return therefore to the
question raised at the beginning before this short historical excursion, why
would a global society tend to operate on a higher, and not merely distinct,
moral level than, say, a national society?

(2)

The reasons, of course, are implicit in the arguments made earlier in regard
to the nation, but now lifted to an entirely new level, that of humanity itself
rather than the citizens of a territorial state. Yet we cannot rest, leaving the
argument merely in this comparative manner. We must explore other aspects
of the claim that we are making. Let us do so by taking up once more the
particular form of knowledge that we call science.

Again we must enter into the debates over universal qualities, in this case
of modern science. There is no question but that modern science emerges in
a context saturated with religious belief and magic. That, collapsing a long
story, it is a social construction, dependent on particular institutions, conventions, and training. It is critical, however, to realize that etiology is not
the same as legitimacy. Once scientific method is established, it must be
judged by its results and its logical coherence rather than by its disorderly

origins. Nor does the fact that science is done by flawed individuals competing for glory, often stumbled upon in serendipitous moments, spurred on by
national or commercial interests that push it in particular directions, etc.
really matter. What matters is that the results of the scientific method (which
vary enormously from field to field in details but circle around common
convictions) are eternally subject to criticism, revision, new formulation,
and downright rejection.[4]

The next thing to be said is that the scientific edifice is always constructed
in terms of particular social structures and historically evolved forms of
social behavior. Yet science makes claims of a universal nature, subject as
they are to constant critical examination. The example already mentioned in
our previous chapter may make this clear. There has been a recent controversy in South Africa over the nature and causes of AIDS and HIV. In terms
of "Western" science, anti-retroviral drugs have been shown to be effective
(though vastly expensive). In the eyes of President Thabo Mbeki and many
of his followers, such drugs are dangerous and merely a form of Western
racism and imperialism. In their place, Mbeki has promoted a South African
drug, Virodene. Takers of this "miracle" drug offer glowing testimonies to
its curative powers. There is no testing of these claims on the Western model,
which is spurned. As one senior African National Congress official is
reported to have said, the HIV model was at best a theory. "Western scientists once said to us the earth was flat. Now we know it's round. I bet one
day we look at AIDS the same way."[5]

What is striking in this account is the lack of knowledge about scientific
method. At the heart of the findings of science, of course, is theory. Such
theory is related to empirical data, and always open to rebuttal. But until
then it is not "mere" theory. It is a piece of universal knowledge. How do we
know the earth is round except by the very science that is being scorned?
There is no Jewish science or South African science. There is only a form of
knowledge (subject, of course, to the tests outlined above) that tries to rise
above tribal or racial diatribes and to proffer its findings as valid for all
human beings.

In speaking about scientific knowledge I have in mind what can be called
both high and low science, i.e., highly theoretical and more or less everyday
science. The former might be something as arcane as quantum physics, the
latter as mundane as knowing what sort of seeds appeal to finches. Most
science is in between. A typical example on the low end of the spectrum
might be the findings resulting from the explorations of the fifteenth century,
in this case by Western seamen. Their newly described geography then
became incorporated into a global system of scientific knowledge, served by
innovations in astronomy, celestial navigation, time devices, meteorological
observations, and so forth. Another more middling example might be
Linnaeus' classification of species. It allowed naturalists all over the world to
identify specimens under a common nomenclature and according to specific

features (of course this system was subject to continued revision and improvement).

I have taken my examples from Western discoveries, where my knowledge is more deeply entrenched. Examples from Chinese and Islamic science in earlier centuries than the fifteenth or the eighteenth could have been selected instead, or as well. The point is that whenever and wherever it emerges, such knowledge enters into the common heritage of humankind in the form of science constantly open to extension and revision. Such knowledge carries with it claims to universality.

Technology can and did in the past have a life separate from science and certainly divorced from high theory. This is less and less the case in modern times. Today the line between pure and applied science becomes more and more porous. A prime example is electronics, where the boundaries between so-called science and engineering are constantly being erased. As the material embodiment of this marriage in, say, computers and the Internet, the result-ing information revolution binds people ever more closely together. The Silk Route linked people intermittently by trade. The silicon chips of today link them directly and instantaneously. One result is that via TV bouncing off satellites in space, we "see" in common the world that we are increasingly inhabiting together, on a daily basis. What I have just said is, of course, a commonplace observation. It needs to be said repeatedly, however, that the surge in communicative action underpins humanity's growth into a possible moral community.

We need to think of science, i.e., the acquisition of knowledge, as rooted in the need of human beings to survive in a physical and social environment where instinct no longer suffices. Such knowledge, developed and refined over many generations, becomes a common inheritance, transmitted by non-genetic means. Local in origin, spotty in its spread, marked by the culture in which it operates, it is nevertheless universal in its aspirations. In its modern manifestations, such science is not only universal as an ideal but increasingly universal in its presence in our everyday, phenomenological lives. As such, it becomes both a bond between people and a universal stratum on which morality, I am arguing, can root itself and find a material basis from which it can flourish in an increasingly global form.

(3)

Science embodies a form of reason. Such reason, though often rarified, is "common." It binds people everywhere in a shared way of reasoning and a common fund of such reasoning's results. It is universal both in its claims and in its practices. As such, it composes a firm underpinning to what today, therefore, we can think of in terms of a global civilization, i.e., a mental universe, shared by all. In this formulation we can then think of local cul-tures, the particular embedding of various other kinds of knowledges that are embraced by bounded groups, as co-existing within this overarching, global civilization.

Yet a moment's reflection suggests that human beings do not live by reason alone. There must be another kind of universality if we are to have people living together in terms of one globe and a common humanity. I refer to sentiment. Often scorned by reason, it is an essential part of human connectivity. As one author puts it nicely, it functions as a "universalizing mode that imagines the possibility of transcending particularity by recognizing a common and shared humanity."[6] Earlier, I mentioned Haskell's piece on how nineteenth-century bourgeois came to feel for the woes of others, about whom they had suddenly acquired intense and immediate knowledge. The knowledge would not have been enough without the sentiment of common humanity that put it into action.

In that same nineteenth century, sentiment was expressed in the form of sympathy, rooted in the nervous system of all humans; or so it was alleged in many quarters. In any case, sympathy, it was claimed, could cross the chasm of class difference. Fellow-feeling could bind up the woes of the poor and oppressed. In fact, as I have argued elsewhere, sympathy was not enough.[7] It needed to be combined with science, in this case in the form of social science, to aspire to be effective. As it turned out, such social science was often as much a matter of ideological statements as of true knowledge. None the less, the ideal was held aloft. It is more often realized in relation to the natural sciences than in the social sciences—anti-retroviral drugs are effective—but not impossible in regard to the latter. In fact, the natural and the social slide together and at best operate synchronously in fostering the betterment of humanity.

In any case, reason must always seek the support of sentiment. As we seek to survive in regard to our natural and social environment, we must now recognize that it is a global environment, knit together by the scientific and technological achievements of the information revolution. In this environment, we find our "location" not only by a global positioning system but by means of our everyday habits. When I go on e-mail, I am in touch, potentially, with "everyman" simultaneously and regardless of his/her physical and territorial local being. Such a binding does not eliminate other ties. Neighborhood associations still exist, we send our children to "local" schools, we recognize others in the supermarkets wherein we shop, and so forth. What has changed is their "location" in our lives, where we have added new and more "disembodied" ties. These ties are increasingly rooted in a common science and a sentiment that transcends our local differences and reminds us of our shared humanity.

(4)

Universalizing science and sentiment foster a sense of what it is to be a "human," who is also a part of humanity. Head and heart must conspire in this conviction. Humanity, in fact, is not something given. We can now see that it is a construct. It is a form of self-awareness that has taken centuries to emerge, and has gone through many historical vicissitudes. It is an abstraction and a reification of relatively recent date. Questions do remain, of course. For example, how characteristic is it of various cultures and civilizations? Is the same concept to be found in China, in India? What are its synonyms? What are the differences from its usage in the West? These are research questions that will broaden our understanding of the concept, but should not affect our basic conclusions.

Merely acknowledging here the possible qualifications involved in treating of the concept in a Western context, let us proceed.[8] What we gain from modern science is the notion of a species, *Homo sapiens*. This, in its simplest terms, is what humanity "is." We "know" this fact as a result of the modern disciplines of anthropology, evolutionary biology, and related inquiries. *This* humanity emerged into the light of day somewhere around the eighteenth to nineteenth century, and mainly in the West. Then it became potentially a possession of all humanity.

But this humanity of which we speak goes back long before the advent of *Homo sapiens* as a conscious identity. Its roots can be found in the Greeks of the fifth century where, though geographically limited in its conception of the "known" world, the notion of a generalized humanity, transcending local boundaries and bounding into the heavens, placed "Man" with the gods. This knowledge was further extended by the Romans, who also pushed forward and extended the earthly territories in which the abstraction "humanity" might find itself. With the decline of the Roman Empire, humanity in the West seemed to absent itself entirely from the earth and to become completely transcendental. In the process, humanity took on a Christian face. It does appear, for example, that in the Christian Middle Ages, Muslims were not viewed in many quarters as part of humanity.

In fact, the awareness of humanity often required an exclusionary principle in which one's enemies were dehumanized. Thus, the other face of humanity was that some beings, whom later times would identify as part of *Homo sapiens*, were not considered human. In the very fifteenth and sixteenth centuries when the sentimental reevocation of the classical world's notion of humanity reached its peak, in the guise of humanism, the dehumanization of American Indians, not to mention Islamic Turks, flourished and formed a constituent part of the definition of humanity itself: its necessary boundary condition.

By the eighteenth century, the notion of humanity as co-existent with all human beings, in principle, was widespread in the West. Associated with cosmopolitanism by the *philosophes*, evocations of humanity were omni-present—and everywhere vague and misty. The term is found frequently in Kant, and equally so in Herder (here, however, it is contrasted with *Volk*, where culture is seen as rooted in the blood, land, and unique history of a particular people). The idea of humanity figures in many titles; typical is the elder Mirabeau's *L'Ami des Hommes*. Here, however, if one looks carefully, Mankind is in fact an eighteenth-century Physiocrat. Yet the aspiration to a universalistic conception is not to be dismissed, for it holds out hope for realization in the future.

Enough hopefully has been said, without continuing at this point the narrative of the concept of humanity, to make convincing the view that humanity is a social and historical construction. By the same token, it should also be clear that *our* task is to understand its meaning in a global epoch, characterized by an information revolution. In carrying out this task, we must pay attention to the role of science/technology as well as the disciplines of the humanities, and to efforts at reasoned understanding as well as to affective and sentimental relations. They help define what it is to be human. At the core of my argument, however, is that the aspirations of the past are now passing into the reality of the present.

In short, humanity is being defined by its creation at this very moment. Everywhere human beings are linked to one another, of course to a greater or lesser degree, in increasingly interconnected and interdependent ways. Traditional and territorial boundaries are transcended by numerous forces: the nuclear threat, the satellites circling overhead, the environmental con-straints illustrated by pictures from those satellites, the MNCs overleaping national restraints on capital and currency, and so forth.

In our global epoch, there are no men or islands unto themselves; nor national sovereignties that, again in theory, can protect anyone accused of "crimes against humanity." That is a new idea. Note that it places political leaders pursuing "inhuman" policies in the ranks of the criminal class. *Human* rights now transcend civic rights. I have tried to show (see Chapter 5) how the latter have been linked to the nation-state, and limited to its cit-izens. It is no accident, therefore, that one of the strongest institutional forces pressing for transcendental, as well as local, rights is the increasing number of INGOs (International Non-Governmental Organizations) and NGOs proliferating around the globe. As their nomenclature tells us, they are non-state, and their claim to rights is not limited by allegiance to a particularistic legal system. Linked globally by the information revolution, the NGOs have become a global force operating frequently in the name of humanity. With all their flaws, and there are many as we have seen, they nevertheless seek to uphold the rights of all peoples, everywhere. In doing so, the NGO may be viewed as making universalistic claims akin to those of science, though of a different sort.

(5)

There is one more piece of the emerging reality of humanity that I want to deal with before finally summarizing the case that globalization brings with it the real possibility of a higher morality. This piece concerns culture. A word of numerous meanings, it, too, like humanity, is an emerging concept of many colors. We sense that there is a unity of some sort to the beliefs, customs, practices, institutions, and way of life of a given group. And that these varied elements have some kind, though of what nature is unclear, of functional relationship to one another. Culture as a term can be applied to primitive societies—groups numbering as little as 50 members—and to modern collectivities of untold numbers. In any case, some sort of culture is assumed to be necessary to hold a group together. Thus we speak of a tribal, a city-state, a national, and now a global culture.

Seeking to avoid the deluge of meanings attached to the word, I want to make a few key points about culture with my thesis in mind. Most scholars have treated the realms of economy, culture, and politics as separate sovereignties. Thus, there are theories as to their contradictory nature, or their growing disjunctures. I want to take the position that we separate these realms at our own risk, for they are merely artificial dikes we erect to keep our knowledges in one area from sloshing over to the next. In reality, of course, there can be no economics that is not part of culture and made possible by culture; no politics separate from economics; nor from culture, and vice-versa.[9] Such a view goes back to the original assertion that the notion of a culture assumes some form of unity. Thus, in focusing here on the cultural aspect of globalization, I insist that it be seen against the backdrop of what I have said about the unity of life and thought.

Having emphasized this point, I want now to make the case that the rise of a global culture *in actuality* is the vital underpinning for the possibility of a higher morality. The evidences for this rise are all around us, in the ubiquitous media representations, in the multinational branding of the world of consumption, in the "ethnic" foods we consume, and in the music we hear. Needless to say, the reception of these artifacts will differ from individual to individual and group to group. That is the necessary distribution curve of global culture, as of any other. Enough is held in common, however, for us to glimpse the emergence of such a global culture.

The word frequently associated with culture is identity. If a global culture is emerging, can we not also imagine a global identity arising? Slowly, hesitantly, in motley coverings, a sense that one is not only a member of a particular family, clan, tribe, state, nation, even international system, but that one is also a member of humanity is making its way forward. There is, therefore, a new sense of self in chrysalis form. A new self-awareness that sees itself as newly human in a way previously only glimpsed in sentimental literature or in transcendental philosophy. Ecce Homo!

Balmurli Natrajan, an anthropologist, has captured what is happening in a very pregnant phrasing. As he remarks, "Globalization . . . transforms the experience of locality itself. . . . Such a transformed experience of the locality is new in the sense of moving us beyond a feeling of 'proximity' (which existed long before globalization due to long-distance trade) to a feeling of 'connectivity', which is dependent upon decreasing . . . 'sociocultural distance' and actually enabling the *cultural* experiences of globalization."[10] It should be noted that such experience is not only enabling, it is also risky, a source of much unease and trepidation as well as exhilaration.

Much of our present-day experience of culture is encapsulated in the term "multiculturalism." However we evaluate this phenomenon, it seems requisite for a global society to accept the cultural particular, as well as its accompanying ethnic and national differences, as part of the very universality of globalization. Equally requisite is the participation of the multi-cultures in the common humanity being made ever more evident by the process of globalization. An essential part of the multicultural must be, and increasingly is, its acknowledgment of the knowledges embodied in what I have earlier described as a global civilization. This is not a foregone conclusion, a teleology, but a dialectical movement manifest in the history around us. Multiculturalism, as part of globalization, is merging into hybridity and creolization, with one result being a mixing of peoples and cultures into a newly constructed "humanity."

(6)

Up to now, I have labored to describe some of the foundations upon which globalization rests. I have sought to depict science/technology as a universalizing force, joining peoples in a common knowledge pool in spite of differences of local cultures. To it must be added sentiments, a sense of solidarity and sympathy with others, again transcending local attachments. Such sentiments held in common take on a universal aspect in the form of an identification with the construct humanity, now no longer a mere aspiration but a reality of everyday life. What can be more real than crimes against humanity? And their trial in international courts? Finally, I spoke of culture and the emergence of a global culture rooted in the factors, and others like them, enumerated above.

Given that the process, or processes, of globalization are pointing in the directions postulated, what are the consequences for morality? I have been arguing that the major outcome is potentially a higher morality. Morality is broadly defined by one dictionary as "the quality of that which conforms to right ideals or principles of human conduct." As we move toward a more universal society—a global one whose interests become identified with those of humanity and not of particular national or ethnic groups—the potential for a higher morality becomes a matter of actual realization. As the dictionary definition un-self-consciously puts it, we should be concerned with *human* conduct. Science, sentiment, and culture all inform us that we face common problems, whether about the environment, economic flows, migration of peoples and ideas, military threats, or human rights. Local solutions, at whatever level, are no longer enough. The new constituency for moral action is humanity itself, constituted on a global scale.

In discussing the postnational constellation, Jürgen Habermas raised the question "whether globalization also affects the cultural substrate of civic solidarity that developed in the context of the nation-state."[11] He, of course, had in mind his earlier work on *The Structural Transformation of the Public Sphere*. In that book he had examined the unique case in which the eighteenth-century European bourgeoisie brought into being what has come to be called civil society. This was a sphere separate from that of state authority. It drew its strength from "public opinion," which in turn appealed to knowledges and truths of a universal nature, held by "humanity." At the end, Habermas was pessimistic, for he believed that the massification of society, its domination by mindless media, and the over-extension of economic interests had eroded the spirit of civic participation in the late twentieth century.

Much of his pessimism was and is justified. I am suggesting, however, that compensatory and emancipatory forces are at work. They are embedded in the constantly emerging nature of globalization, which, with all its negative features—and there are many, as I have repeatedly said—nevertheless holds out promise for a higher morality. The local pursuit of self-interest now has to contend with a new definition of "self." Global climate changes affect all of humanity, not merely one island in the ocean. Moreover, what happens on that one island is now a matter of immediate knowledge to all human-kind. The same is true for a host of other matters, such as human rights. Particular tyrannies, and their local sovereignties, can no longer shield abuses and violations of such rights from universal display and thus potential action to remedy them.

Needless to say, I am pointing to a direction, not to a destiny already arrived at—to a desired state of affairs, whose actual realization will at best be asymptotic, and is at this time only fitful and partial. In the avant-garde of this movement, to use that old-fashioned term, is the increasing number of NGOs. They are in part the new parliaments of humankind, the new repre-sentatives of the human spirit as it aspires to a higher morality. Operating to a large extent in the virtual space of the information revolution, occasionally mustering their forces on the ground, they constitute a new conscience. Its voice speaks globally, and as an alternative to that of existing nation-states. Such NGOs represent a new version of Habermas' public sphere, and comprise a transformation currently in process.

This particular process is part of the larger process taking place under the rubric of globalization. Arising in its present manifestation only within the last half century or so, present-day globalization, certainly in the terms of science/technology, sentiment, and culture that I have focused on, has the potential to move to the music of a higher morality. Whether this potential will be realized, of course, is a matter of much contingency and some in-built tendencies. Critical to the realization of a morality that takes its marching orders from an actual and self-realizing humanity is action and agency. Only if enough of us choose to share a global culture and then behave in accordance with its inspiration will the potential become the actual.

Whatever study of globalization we undertake, we must realize that morality is a crucial part of what must concern us, along with the economic, political, social, and other features that currently get so much attention. We must also constantly bear in mind that we are talking of a process that may take centuries, certainly many decades, as it unfolds. In the end, the major importance of globalization will probably reside in its bringing into being a global consciousness, at whose core is the idea of a newly constructed humanity. Continued study of this fact, for such it is becoming, can play a major, constituent role in further bringing it into actuality.

Chapter 9

Global Humanity

In tackling the issue of morality as it relates to globalization, and vice-versa, I have repeatedly used the term humanity. It is time for additional reflection on the meaning of this term. It is interesting, for example, to ask when the word, and the idea, of "humanity" comes into existence? To answer this question, I have been arguing that it is a social construct, an imaginary community, emerging through historical vicissitudes as a form of self-awareness. In the terms in which I am addressing it, the notion of "human-ity" is a recent invention, a novel conception, whose existence is correlated with the ending of World War II and the beginning of the present-day pro-cess of globalization. The tribunals following upon WW II attempt to define humanity legally; the processes of globalization give actuality to the notion of a common humanity.

Surely, however, I am making a hyperbolic argument. Has not humanity existed since the dawn of human time, that is, the evolution of the species *Homo sapiens*? Has it not been present in Greek and Roman times, as when Terence declares that "Nothing human is alien to me"? Does it not flower in the eighteenth-century Enlightenment, where numerous books and tracts have the word humanity in their titles? Does it not appear full blown in Hegel's ruminations? And what of the notion in non-Western societies, where it takes particularistic but nevertheless recognizable and comparable form.

Again, the question of humanity has taken on new salience and meaning in the last half of the twentieth century and into the new millennium. New forces have been and are at work—our present vicissitudes—bringing into being humanity as a new imaginary, which is exercising its powers in a new actuality.

As we saw in Chapter 3, the Nuremberg trials took the major step of moving from mere war crimes, as defined by existing codes, to what were declared to be "crimes against humanity." It redefined aggressive war as a crime against the world, and invited individuals to answer to their own consciences—and thus humanity—in refusing to obey the orders of their leaders. Hartley Shawcross, one of the prosecuting lawyers, argued that the

accused had engaged in a campaign of deception, treachery, and murder—
"How can any of them now say he was not a party to common murder in its
most ruthless forms?"—and that their trial "must form a milestone in the
history of civilization."[1]

"Crimes against *humanity*": this was an idea whose time had come, no
matter how hedged in by the old terms of internationalism. First apparently
used at the time of the massacres of Armenians in 1915, it emerged as if
de novo at the time of WW II.[2] It meant that leaders could be seen as
illegitimate because they fostered "inhuman" behavior. Such behavior, as
described in various declarations and Tribunal charges, included "murder,
extermination, enslavement, deportation or forcible transfer of populations,
imprisonment, torture, rape, sexual slavery, enforced prostitution, forced
pregnancy and enforced sterilization, persecution, enforced disappearances,
apartheid, and other inhumane acts."[3] This is a long list, and controversy
can arise over the interpretation of any one of the charges. The current
debate over torture in the United States is a case in point. Partly this is
because the implication in such a matter is that a positive judgment could
transcend national sovereignty; it would be made in the name of humanity,
with punishment to be carried out by humanity as the plaintiff.[4]

Unfortunately in my view, from the beginning another term, "genocide,"
was tied to the notion of crimes against humanity, thereby limiting its scope.
During the war, Winston Churchill, reacting to what he viewed as the
unprecedented Nazi murders, commented that "We are in the presence of a
crime without a name." In response, a Polish Jew and legal expert, Raphael
Lemkin, whose family had been victims of the Nazis, introduced the term
"genocide" in 1944 to describe the horrible happenings. He then campaigned
for an international treaty making such practice criminal and subject to
punishment. In 1948, the UN General Assembly adopted a law banning it,
followed by a Genocide Convention.[5]

Thus, the crime against humanity that had no name had now acquired
one: genocide. This was a very positive step. For Lemkin, however, who had
certain ideological predilections, genocide was defined as not only killing
people but eliminating their whole way of life and culture. Thus, as one
scholar, Gerard Alexander, puts it, "genocide is defined as an attempt
to destroy communities defined in religious, ethnic or cultural terms."
Excluded from the treaty banning genocide were attempts "to destroy
groups defined in political terms."[6] Thus, the Soviet Gulag, or the Maoist
mass murders, not being defined as genocides, escaped under the radar identifying crimes against humanity. So, too, the power of the international
covenanting powers to intervene in the name of humanity, transcending
national boundaries in so doing, was severely limited in cases of terrible
inhuman oppressions that were not defined as genocide.

(1)

Such language is now anachronistic. Equality is a cornerstone of the conception of humanity. Manifesting itself specifically in the form of human rights, it insists on everyone—women, children, minorities and not just male members—being equally entitled to what were formerly the privileges of one set and sex. John Stuart Mill referred to this change as the "Domestic Revolution," implicitly comparing it to the French Revolution. The drive to equality, obviously, has deep roots: in religions of various sorts, in the secular philosophies of the Enlightenment, even in the all-pervasive nature of consumerism. This drive has gathered speed and spread ever more widely. To be found in such venues as bibles and novels, the aspiration to various forms of equality has leaped across time and space via the new media and the Internet. Institutionalized in many NGOs, it insists that everyone, not just everyman, has rights because of belonging to humanity and not to a particular country and its legal system. Not everywhere triumphant, or accepted to the same degree, the notion that everyone is equal in the sense of belonging to humanity, and vice-versa, is nevertheless a powerful and prevalent characteristic of our time.

I am arguing throughout this book that to see this shift requires a whole new view. Humanity today is being defined in terms of the happenings of globalization. It is being formed by factors such as satellite communication, linking humans everywhere to a previously unknown degree— by the threat of nuclear annihilation; by the common danger of irreversible environmental damage, resulting from human actions; by the multiplication of MNCs and NGOs, made possible by the satellite and computer links; and by a host of similar factors involved in present-day globalization.[7]

The process of imagining Humanity gathers force from these factors and from something called by the philosopher Ian Hacking "dynamic nominalism." This means, we are told, that "once you invent a category—as, for example, the category of 'homosexual' seems to have been invented in the late nineteenth century—people will sort themselves into it, behave according to the description, and thus contrive new ways of being."[8] As the category "humanity" takes on greater imaginative power and existence, it attracts people into it, and swells the category itself. Perhaps another way to describe this process is to speak of a self-fulfilling prophecy. The notion of a category and its realization, however, give a firmer epistemological footing to the project. The notion of Humanity becomes more and more a self-realizing "destiny" for the species that used to be called Mankind.

(2)

At the most fundamental level, humanity is a matter of biology cum culture. A few comments will promote our discussion. The great classifier Carl

Linnaeus was the first to introduce the term "Homo sapiens," doing so in the tenth edition of his *Systema Naturae* in 1758. Placing the species under Mammalia and then Primates, the Swedish naturalist brought home the fact that Man was an animal, to be studied as one. This study was still set in the context of the two-thousand-year-old belief in the Great Chain of Being—a vision of a hierarchical world reaching from God to the tiniest entity, in which each species and each individual was related to all the rest as either "above" or "below."[9] Clearly this was a static conception. Once it was replaced by Darwin's theory of evolution by natural selection, *Homo sapiens* could be conceived of as having a history.

Linnaeus had taken one of the first steps that would eventuate in Darwin and evolutionary biology. The Swedish naturalist also, however, separated man from man, by introducing racial distinctions. Thus, he pursued his rage for classification by speaking of Wild Man, American, European, Asiatic and African, with the implicit and often explicit claim that the European was superior and the American and African inferior. Still, the fundamental unity of humanity was implicit in the umbrella term *Homo sapiens*, generally interpreted as "wise man."[10]

Thus was created the biological category for imagining Humanity in scientific terms. Set in the discourse of the Great Chain of Being, human beings were placed below the angels but above the other primates such as apes and chimps. Well before Linnaeus the resemblance of humans and apes was a commonplace observation. Even the groundlings of Shakespeare's time knew what he had in mind when he has Othello utter the words, "I would change my Humanity with a Baboone."[11] Self-definition is almost always in terms of what one is not: to be human is to aspire to be an angel and to recognize that one is not an ape. Thus, humanity seeks to separate itself from the bestial.

Yet, with the work of Darwin, that separation became harder to make in some ways, while easier in others. Physical anthropology and evolutionary biology showed in detail how connected Man and the other primates were. Now there was a different chain, one which linked chimps to their collateral branches, and which produced early man in his various modes—*Australopithecus, Homo habilis, Homo erectus* and then *Homo sapiens*. A major difference between the latter and chimps and gorillas was in the larger jaws and smaller brains of these simian cousins. The fossil record tracks the evolution into *Homo* that began about 2.3 million years ago, beginning the long trek toward what I am identifying today as Humanity.

(3)

In that journey, *Homo sapiens* became wise mainly because of what we have come to call culture. Thus if the basis of Humanity is the biological evolution that I have briefly touched upon, its exfoliation is in terms of cultural evolution. The record of that evolution is to be found in terms of history rather more than in fossils. It is this evolution that I have in mind when I speak of the historical vicissitudes, culminating for the moment in the process of present-day globalization.

It is a long story, often told today in the form of World History. Throughout its existence, *Homo sapiens* remains an animal. Its nature is rooted, as sociobiology keeps telling us, in its genes, so closely resembling those of its cousinly primates. So are human social relations. In the case of chimps, as we now know, they live in groups, inhabiting a specific territory, which they defend against others. They compete for females (and, in fact, vice-versa, with the female competition for males perhaps less obvious), kill chimps from neighboring communities, and seek to expand their territories; and so forth.[12] Not unexpectedly, we find similar traits in humans.

Any attempt to describe human nature must reckon with these facts, and how they are mirrored in human behavior. In seeking to understand the social construction of Humanity, we must recognize these foundations. Man's inhumanity is a constant part of his humanness, as exemplified in the story of Cain and Abel. *Homo sapiens* is a covetous, murderous, conniving beast of prey. To say this, however, is to give only half the story. As Thomas Huxley understood in his *Evolution and Ethics*, the species is in conflict with nature, seeking to deny its competitive nature and to aspire to something "higher." In the conflict described by Huxley, *Homo sapiens'* base and basic instincts must be hedged around by barriers and restraints. These must be of both a legal and a cultural/social nature. It is in this context that I wish to place what I have been saying about morality and globalization.

In fact, that something "higher" is also rooted in humanity's genetic evolution, as the species moves toward cultural evolution. Huxley's mentor, Charles Darwin, had already recognized that altruism was as much a part of human nature as narrow self-interest and preservation. In his account in the *Descent of Man*, Darwin seeks to show how man is lifted, so to speak, above himself by the rise of social conscience and religion. That book is a good place to begin a study of the civilizing process, though the author of the *Descent* does not himself operate in those terms.

Once gifted by the evolutionary process with language and the ability to manipulate symbols, the species can imagine a past, present, and future. It can aspire to a self-realization, rooted in its own spiritual aspirations. In a long-drawn-out and non-deterministic process, often in the form of two steps forward and one step back, *Homo sapiens* has been moving toward an ever wider sense of community. One version was envisioned in the eighteenth century, for example, by Immanuel Kant, whose name I have invoked earlier. The German philosopher spoke of the "cosmopolitan nature" of Mankind, which leads the species in a transcendental direction. We ourselves can think in more dynamic and less teleological terms. Mankind has no fixed nature—there is no human nature as such, only a changing, kaleidoscopic set of characteristics, based as they are on certain evolutionary tendencies. Indeed, as I am arguing, the species is struggling *in* history—the historical vicissitudes referred to earlier—to define itself.

(4)

If evolutionary theory tells us about human nature, an empirical matter, it tells us little or nothing about human rights, a normative subject (treated at some length in Chapter 5). The latter is a product of cultural evolution, which we know about basically as a matter of historical experience. In the case of human rights, it is a recent experience. It can be traced back, in the West, to roots in natural law theory. With the Dutch philosopher Hugo Grotius, the concept of human rights took a momentous step forward in the seventeenth century when he defined them as separable from God's will. As such they became intrinsically *human*, with humans conceiving of them in contractual terms. As Lynn Hunt argues persuasively, it required revolutions to bring such rights into actuality.[13]

It is worth repeating part of the story. The great revolutions in the West at the end of the eighteenth century enshrined human rights in the form of declarations. What had previously been the privileges of the few now became the rights of the many. Where privileges had formerly been attached to individuals as members of an estate or a guild, now they were declared the birthright of any individual who was a member of the nation. Such at least they were in principle. In practice, women and minorities were excluded from the entitlements of the "rights of man." When the French entitled their Declaration that of the Rights of Man and Citizen, they indicated the gender and political limits to the so-called human rights. Hence the paradox of a universal declaration with local restrictions.

Still, an expanded version of humanity and human rights had been given to the world. To cite Lynn Hunt again, the Revolution indicated "the depth of the challenge that human rights posed to hierarchical societies based on privilege and birth and the continuing challenge they offer to inequality, injustice, and despotic authority of all kinds."[14] Fenced in as that challenge was by the eighteenth-century declarations, it served as inspiration for those who wished to expand rights to all of humanity, and not just members of particular states.

The shift, of course, did not take place all at once. Hegel marks one way station in regard to theory. Wrestling mightily with redefinitions of freedom and self, the German philosopher sought to go beyond his compatriot Kant, and the latter's exhortation to his Enlightenment colleagues to "Dare to Know." Hegel, instead, threw out the challenge to "Dare to Know thyself" (my words), that is, to critique one's own self as historically developed and developing.[15] As part of this development, as explained by Hegel in his *Philosophy of Right* (note the last word in the title) in 1821, "It is part of education, of thinking as the consciousness of the single in the form of universality, that the ego comes to be apprehended as a universal person in which all are identical. A man counts as a man in virtue of his manhood alone, not because he is a Jew, Catholic, Protestant, German, Italian, &c. This is an assertion which thinking ratifies, and to be conscious of it is of infinite importance."[16]

Hegel, as is well known, having glimpsed a promised land, faltered and lapsed into parochialism and provincialism, or at best extreme Eurocentrism.[17] His reiterated use of the term "man" as what counts, though it reaches out to a larger conception, shows the partiality of his time and vision. Yet, when posed against the announcement, say, of the contemporary Savoyard/Frenchman Joseph de Maistre that "I have seen, in my life, Frenchmen, Italians, Russians, ... but as to man, I declare never to have met him in my life," we recognize how far Hegel has come.[18] He has posited a consciousness—a self-consciousness—that needed only to come down from the abstract spaces of his philosophy into the actuality of human existence to give substance to the category Humanity.

Jumping from Hegel to our own times, we note the pronounced shift from civic and national to human rights, mediated by the German philosopher's recognition of man as a being conscious of his humanity. That shift, for us, was correlative with the war crimes trials of WW II and the expansion of globalization, bringing more and more peoples closer and closer. The declaration of rights by the UN in 1948 marks the difference from earlier, more limited declarations. The rights listed here are for all people and not just for those in particular nation-states. Deficient as to enforcement, vague as to economic and social protections, the 1948 declaration none the less is animated by a sense that the idea, or fact, of Humanity confers rights that transcend local cultures and societies.

The establishment of an International Criminal Court was subsequently as important as the declaration. This tribunal, established by the 1998 Treaty of Rome, set up punishments for those who violated human rights. There have been many failures in all of these early efforts to promote human rights. The trial of Slobodan Milosevic was stretched over four years, and was still inconclusive at the moment of his death. The genocide of Rwanda was not prevented, and the punishments for its perpetuators hardly serve as a model of judicial procedures. Sudanese violations of human rights, perhaps to the point of genocide, have left over a million people homeless; again the international community has been laggard if not criminal in its neglect to do something. Yet, such failures must not be allowed to obscure the fact that human rights are actually and positively on the agenda of Humanity. For example, Kosovo has hardly been an unmitigated success, but it can and should be seen as the first war for human rights, a remarkable transcending of national sovereignty in the *name implicitly* of Humanity.

(5)

Humanity is global. It inhabits space. Human beings are local. They live in specific places. Crimes against humanity are also crimes against particular human beings. Murder, torture, and slavery take place in a territory occupied by women, children and men who are individuals, as well as members of a tribe, ethnicity or nation—and also of humanity. (And we must remember that territory is itself an historically defined entity.) The actual victims of crimes against Humanity are Bosnians, Rwandans, and Sudanese; they, not Humanity as such, suffer in their bodies and minds, as they are caught up in global processes, of the break-up or construction of nations, of the global traffic in arms, or of the resultant refugee and migration problems. Thus, they experience these happenings in their own lives, not as mere history. This fact must never be forgotten. Nevertheless, it must not be allowed to obscure for us the additional fact that the local is also always global; indeed, the two are elided. What is new as a result of present-day globalization is that the elision is narrowing. The two—global and local—are becoming more and more intertwined, as a reality and not a mere abstract notion.

In this reality, differences among peoples remain. They have different cultures. These will not vanish. The various cultures, however, will all take on more and more global components. It is clear that this is what is happening today. Distances are shrinking. It does seem true that there is a strong tendency, universally, for peoples in societies to be reluctant "to conceive outsiders in the same terms as themselves." Thus, in the past many languages have had "no term for 'human being' except that used to denote speakers of the language concerned."[19] Today, while different cultures and languages persist, as they should, it seems hard to imagine any that will continue to deny the appellation "human" to others with a good conscience. Robert Burns' appeal for someone to "give us the giftie/To see ourselves as others see us," becomes more and more difficult to deny in front of our television screens and computer monitors.

Analytically, the assertion of a "common humanity" can be attacked on the grounds that it can cover over differences in power and situation.[20] Attention must be given to the dangers inherent in this matter. The cure, however, is not to abandon the notion of Humanity, suitably hedged in by pragmatic considerations, but to bring the ideal and the reality, the global and the local, closer to one another. And this is exactly what globalization is doing as a matter of fact, We are, admittedly, only at the beginning of what is an asymptotic process at best, but the awareness of belonging to a common species, historically forging its way toward common rights, is part of the realization of the ideal, partial as this may be. Without the ideal—a sort of utopia or no place—Humanity would be hampered in its quest to place itself in a new space and time.

(6)

What I have tried to show is that the frame in which any such observations and questions fit is provided by the introduction into history of the term *Homo sapiens*. A classification which gives biological unity to Mankind, it became the basis for theories about evolution, which process took a turn to the cultural about 40,000 years ago. This then provides the ground on which ideational unity concerning Humanity has been able to arise. It takes the form of self-awareness and emerges through the vicissitudes of history. In its latest manifestation as historical consciousness, that is, going back about 2,500 years, this consciousness—especially in the form of history per se— now allows us to be aware that we are involved in a process of increased globalization; and that one of the consequences of globalization is that we are *actually* becoming something called Humanity and not merely aspiring toward that state.

A self-reinforcing process is under way, in which aspiration and reality mingle in a more and more interconnected manner. In the end, we must understand that Humanity is a continuing project, very incomplete as yet, and subject to great stresses and strains, of both mind and matter. The implications of this project for morality are fundamental, not merely in the abstract but as a practical matter in everyday life. Once we are fully aware that we are part of Humanity, we can act more forcefully as complete human beings, accepting the "inhuman" part of our being and constraining it in an increasingly humane and institutionalized fashion. Such may be the future of Global Humanity.

Conclusion

There are many ways to seek an understanding of globalization. In this book, I am arguing for one such way: the application of an historical perspective, which I am labeling the New Global History. Employing this perspective, I have sought to deal with particular aspects of present-day globalization: my intent is to illustrate how this perspective can operate. Thus I hope to contribute both to a general discourse surrounding the subject as well as to further research and thought concerning what I like to call the "factors" of the contemporary globalization process.

In attaching the adjective "historical" to what I am doing, I do not mean to restrict the approach to the discipline of history as such. In fact, the New Global History must include the insights and work of the other social science disciplines as well as those aspects of the humanities and the natural sciences that can bear on the topic. The phrase "multidisciplinary" is, in fact, better suited to what we are talking about.

Still, I believe that history is the context in which work on globalization best takes place. Only history, in my view, allows and fosters the attempt at a holistic view of the subject. Its very lack of a general theory or particular "laws" becomes its strength. The historian seeks to do research and thinking on the pieces and then aims at interpreting them in terms of their interrelations with one another. In the end the historian sees that the connected pieces form something that he/she calls globalization. In doing this, the historian mirrors the synchronicity and synergy of the factors of the globalization process itself. I am arguing for a redefined history, however, a challenge not always appreciated by the guild members of the discipline (of which I am one).[1]

The irony, of course, is that historians have generally lagged behind other social scientists in seeking to understand present-day globalization. Economists, sociologists, and anthropologists have been there before them. Political scientists and international relations people have arrived at about the same time. This is partly why New Global History must be multi-, or at least inter-, disciplinary in its approach. A besetting sin of global studies, however, is that the disciplines are too frequently cordoned off from one another, becoming barriers to intellectual exchange rather than facilitators. Each discipline, naturally, has its own scholarly journals. They increasingly carry articles on globalization. A glance at these articles, alas, shows little or no cross-referencing to work done in other disciplines. It is as if the interdependence and interconnectivity of globalization has not penetrated to the disciplines that seek to study the process.

The existing social science disciplines all emerged more or less from the challenges thrown up by the French and Industrial revolutions. Called forth to help in our understanding of the new world of life and thought of the last few hundred years, they have served resolutely. The problem is that they now need to change, in ways that are still not clear. Where they originated in a world dominated by emerging nation-states, set in an international system, we now face a world in which the nation-state, while still of immense power, is confronted by forces transcending its boundaries and abilities. While the setting of the social sciences has hitherto been that of an industrializing world, ours has shifted to an information society, operating to a great extent in virtual space, characterized by a new time/space compression. Amidst all the other changes brought about by globalization, we need to add those required by the disciplines and their practitioners.[2]

Needless to say, this puts a strain on them. Globalization provokes anxiety in daily life; it also does so in our intellectual pursuits. Paradoxically, New Global History, while it may give rise to anxiety in our lives and professional careers, also has the potential to quell such feelings. It offers a way of giving us understanding that allows us to take our existing strengths and dedications and use them in the service of achieving new knowledge. Such knowledge serves to "re-place" ourselves in the emerging global world that increasingly makes up our lives. Knowledge is power: power to orient ourselves properly in a new epoch and a new space, and thereby to quiet our anxieties.

Part of that reorientation is the recognition that globalization is not simply a product of the West but results from the interplay of many nations and peoples. Thus, New Global History takes its place with World History and Global History per se as part of the effort to transcend the Eurocentric perspective. Multinational corporations and non-governmental organizations are to be found everywhere in the world. The UN, the World Bank, the IMF are basically global institutions (though serious imbalances in the strength of those running these groups is clearly present). The Internet and World Wide Web connect the entire globe (although again differentially). Peoples, too, are increasingly intermixed, affected by global processes and by physical movement: diasporas, refugees, and population and labor shifts, for example, are all partial consequences of the factors of globalization and their interactions.

As a truly global happening, the subject of our study puts a further strain on our parochial knowledges. In addition to transcending disciplinary boundaries, we must now also transcend all sorts of other cultural (and political and social) boundaries. China and India must be as close to us in all sorts of ways as Europe and America. Perhaps only team efforts can cope with the expanding demands that globalization places upon us as we attempt to achieve knowledge about it. It is in this light, incidentally, that one might wish to look at the spread of English as the *lingua franca* (*franca*, an anachronism?), facilitating greater communication.

Fortunately, the processes of globalization themselves foster a trans-Western perspective on the subject. For example, frequent conferences, made easier by the increased speed of transportation systems, bring together students of the topic from all parts of the world. Representing different traditions and takes in regard to globalization, these students are forced to try to reconcile different points of view. East does meet West and, to an ever greater extent, North meets South. So, too, geography itself is up for grabs, as territory takes on new meaning in a global epoch.[3] This is made palpably clear when scholarly exchange takes place via the Internet. The sender's address is in virtual space, not a physical location. Of course mind is still shaped by "national" and "cultural" forces specific to place; but increasingly mind is flying free from its "local" ties.

Thus, the perspective of New Global History itself seeks to become global. Realism requires us to point out that human beings can and probably should only partially free themselves from their more "traditional" locations. Such realism also causes us to admit that much of what has been said so far is hortatory, positing an ideal to which we should aspire. We must also admit that whatever closing of the gap between ideal and reality occurs will also be asymptotic. Still, it is critically important that the direction be made clear.

(1)

Because I am trying to present a new perspective, with selected illustrations, I have necessarily neglected or scanted various parts of the globalization *problematique*. This book does not aspire to be an encyclopedia of globalization, the last word on the subject. It will be useful, however, if I indicate some of the omissions, so that others may inquire further into them. (In some cases, I myself have explored them more intensively elsewhere; I will cite such work in the notes.) In short, I am suggesting that the overview and methodology proposed here be used to reexamine various thematic components of global history in greater detail and depth.

After WW II, what has come to be called World History arose as a reaction to previous national and Eurocentric work. In place of the standard survey course on the history of European civilization or, more broadly, Western civilization, courses came into being on the history of the whole world, or, as sometimes said, the rest of the world. Institutions in the form of journals, associations, conferences, websites, etc., sprang into existence. Publishers employed the rubric "World History" under which to group a disparate set of books. Guardian angels, so to speak, were Oswald Spengler and Arnold J. Toynbee, with the latter strongly influencing William McNeill, recognized by many as the father of world history. Under his aegis, and that of numerous colleagues, world history departed from its original practitioners and took on more concrete features, paying much attention to cross-border phenomena, such as plagues, population movements, environmental pressures, and related subjects.

At about the same time something called Global History arose as a post-WW II attempt to transcend the limited national and European perspectives employed in doing history. Confusion also arose. Were World and Global History synonyms, as some have contended? If not, what were the differences? Or were they simply on a spectrum, with overlaps preventing any clear distinction? Various scholars espouse each of these positions.[4]

My starting point in these debates is to remember that the word "globalization" is of relatively recent vintage: somewhere around the 1960s–1970s.[5] Once coined, then the neologism could be read backwards into history. One could then seek earlier episodes, phases, stages—what have you—of what we could now recognize as leading to increased interconnection and interdependence of peoples. In this light, there seemed to be a direction of sorts in history, toward increased globalization, though advancing intermittently and sporadically. Over all of this the specter of "progress" hovered.

World history, in this view, seemed to be the deep reservoir from which one could dredge up the monster of globalization. Global historians could focus on this one theme as it made its way through time and human experience. On this account, World and Global History are not synonyms but siblings, at best, with the occasional rivalry that characterizes such relations. Both, of course, are efforts to transcend the limitations of previous Western-centric histories, and to cope with the post-1945 world.

Where does New Global History fit into this story? As I have suggested earlier, the adjective "New" was only grudgingly applied to Global History. This came about to mark what I and various colleagues see as a "rupture" of sorts, occurring in the past half century and pressing on even more vigorously into the new millennium. I have tried to spell out many of the details of this rupture in this book. It can, of course, be debated whether a rupture has actually taken place. Scholars of the French Revolution have faced the same problem. Were the events of 1789 merely a continuation of trends already in existence or did the Revolution mark a sharp break? De Tocqueville, for example, saw much of the Revolution in the Old Regime itself. In addition, he carried the Revolution's espousal of democracy forward into the New World and America. Something similar can be done today with globalization.

Continuity or break? In the perspective I am advancing, I have opted for the latter as the more fitting description. Continually, I have insisted that the post-WW II factors of globalization are rooted in earlier developments: there is continuity. But just as strongly I have been arguing that continuity should not be allowed to obscure the profound change represented by contemporary globalization. There are jumps in the existence of human beings, systemic and holistic changes that make for a new era, a new epoch. Such jumps encompass shifts both in the material surround of *Homo sapiens* and in the species' consciousness. It is such a period, I am arguing, through which human beings have been and are now passing. By using the adjective "New," I have sought to call attention to this profound transformation and, along with other scholars, to mark it out as a field for research.

(2)

It is because of this view that I am not attempting to cover what others have done so well elsewhere. With this position established—and it is why I have given so much attention to what is otherwise a parochial disciplinary discussion—I can now say a few words more about what else is not in this book. These are all proper topics for work in New Global History, which I cite so that others may address them with the perspective being advanced here. Each can be said to deserve at least a chapter and possibly a separate book on its own. Here I will mention them only briefly, as part of a list. I do so even though it may appear counterproductive to highlight the book's shortcomings and gaps (in fact some are alluded to several times in the main text); but I am willing to run that risk in the interest of the fullest possible picture of the field's research possibilities.

Imperialism and colonialism are two such topics. Both imperialism and colonialism are part of the expansion of globalization, breaking down established barriers and creating increased interconnectivity.[6] Scholars in each of these fields have moved with some ease toward World and Global History, and even in a few cases toward New Global History. Imperialism, especially, as it branches into cultural imperialism, becomes an important part of present-day globalization.[7] Arguments abound as to whether economic hegemony, as with the USA, should be seen as the contemporary form of imperialism. In such arguments, the question of the difference between colonialism, as territorial expansion, and imperialism, as a matter of hegemony exercised in many shapes, becomes important.

Americanization is another topic that should be on any list of important issues in contemporary globalization. Sometimes it forms part of the discussion on imperialism, other times it is directly situated in talk about the central role of free-market economics. Implicit in such a discussion is the question as to whether the world is headed in the direction of increased homogeneity. My own view is that this discussion should be in terms of how much homogenization and how much heterogeneity are taking place in the process, and in what particular ways and in what particular areas. Instead of a black-white assertion, what is needed is empirical work (paying much attention, for example, to multinational corporations and their "location"). America plays a role, but surely the assertion of Americanization runs counter to the thrust of globalization, which is a many-factored, multinational process.

I have already mentioned diasporas, refugee problems, and population and labor movements. These, too, can demand independent and extensive treatment. When this is accorded, it should be with an eye to the connection of these topics with the other factors highlighted in our analysis of the process of globalization. It might be well to be aware that regionalism may be as appropriate a frame as globalization in which to place such an examination. Indeed, different frames—the national, the regional, and the global—may each reveal a different picture of what is happening. Here, too, we should look at the ways in which the national and the regional relate overall to the process of globalization itself.[8]

Culture is a term hard to define. Yet it is clearly central to any analysis such as our present one. I have already mentioned cultural imperialism. With culture itself the emphasis might be on the way the informational revolution and the new means of instantaneous communication, unshackled by government restrictions (or at least seeking to circumvent them), are bringing people and peoples together into a global process. For my part, I would seek to stress the global/local aspect of the cultural approach: global culture takes on a local look, and local culture becomes globalized (this has already been adumbrated in some of the earlier chapters). In a similar vein, as argued earlier, the disciplines that we bring to bear on our studies are not sharply divided into culture and economics, or culture and politics, or whatever: economics is as much cultural as it is purely economic, and vice-versa. It is only for convenience's sake that we pretend otherwise, and go about our craft inquiries.[9]

Religion, it can be said, has in a sense risen from the dead in the twentieth century. Supposedly buried by the secularizing forces of modernity, it has, to quote one scholar, "re-entered the political and cultural arenas of modern society." Its most dramatic form today, of course, is Islam. As this same scholar continues, religion à la Islam has "become the main vector of transposition of religion from a private or secondary public sphere into the central political arenas and arsenals of collective representation."[10] Obviously, it is not just Islam but religion in general that plays a major role in globalization. It must be aligned with discussions of culture, of emerging identities, of relations to ethnic and national struggles, as we seek to understand what is happening in a global epoch.

Gender also deserves a chapter (indeed, it should run through all the chapters). Here, one would have to break new ground, for the relation of gender to globalization, and vice-versa, is an under-theorized and under-researched topic. In my own tentative efforts at outreach in this regard, I have found a curious unreceptivity on the part of gender scholars. Perhaps they feel they have other battles to fight. In any case, the effort must be made on all sides. One interesting and suggestive probe has been made in regard to World History. Reviewing two books on women's history in a global (actually world) perspective, the reviewer takes inspiration from a comment by Virginia Woolf in 1938: "As a woman, I have no country. As a woman I want no country. As a woman my country is the whole world." In fact, of course, this is a typical expression of cosmopolitanism rather than of a world or global perspective. However, the reviewer goes on to remind us that women are used to viewing their plight as "transcending the borders of the nation" from the nineteenth century on. Thus, they are prime candidates for a world historical, and I would add a new global history, perspective. In regard to the former, we are told that accounts of exploration, trade, imperialism tend to render women invisible at the same time as "such topics as family, reproduction, and sexuality . . . [are] largely neglected."[11] The same, *mutatis mutandis*, can be said of Global and New Global History. It is a situation that needs to be rectified, if we are to see the true shape of globalization today.

There is one last set of topics that beg to be taken up in any work going beyond this book. The major heading would be anti-globalization. Globalization requires a balance sheet. Alongside its achievements, many injustices have and are being practiced in its name. Understandably, resistance and opposition have shown themselves, ranging from anti-McDonald's campaigns, to opposition to the WTO, to more serious uprisings, such as the Zapatistas in Mexico. Groups, including some NGOs, have formed to protest various aspects of globalization seen as nefarious. Anti-globalization, in my view, must be included as an intrinsic part of the globalization process. There is a dialectic involved, with the forces of globalization and anti-globalization changing and challenging each other in significant or trivial ways. The full story must take account of this contestation and exchange.

Risk, and risk assessment, play a large role in any account of globalization.[12] Nuclear disasters, global environmental changes, a global arms market, terrorist activities, all seem to threaten the peaceful expansion of globalization understood as increased interdependence and as a move toward greater peace and justice (*pace* my chapters on morality). What is new about such risks is that they may be irreversible: global warming is a prime example.

The fact is that globalization, like any other piece of history, is a messy, localized development, whose outcomes, as I have stressed repeatedly, are uncertain and contingent. One author uses the term "friction" to describe this aspect.[13] She then exemplifies it in a treatment of the conflict in Indonesia over the landscape, such as forests and streams, between so-called indigenous peoples and developers. Here, global connectiveness takes on lived reality: the particular and universal, the local and global, become immediate parts of individual and collective life. The author's work is a reminder of how globalization actually works on the ground, and how we must seek to understand it empirically and theoretically in all of our research. The challenge is then to incorporate such understanding in the larger understanding of the process of globalization that arises from such "friction."

(3)

In the chapters of this book I have attempted to deal with pieces of the whole of our "global epoch," to give some idea as to how they might fit together, and especially to describe the overall perspective that should be brought to the task. Thus I have tried in the first two chapters to place the New Global History perspective in the frame of past history and in ways of doing that history, ways that link easily to World and Global History. In these chapters I have spoken of "globalization without end," to indicate the way past and present are linked and to assert that there seems to be no foreseeable end to both the process of globalization and the discussions about it. I also attempted to root my own discussion in certain canonical figures—Adam Smith, Karl Marx, and Max Weber, for example—and thus to show that the central concern of globalization—the nature of social relations and the growing interconnectedness of peoples—is the same as that pursued by such earlier thinkers.

Globalization, however, is not a matter merely of thought and theory. It manifests itself in the world in terms of actors and institutions. It takes its rise from happenings in the political, economic, social, and cultural life of individuals and national and ethnic groupings, to mention only a few of the most prominent ones. The chapter on the Cold War, therefore, is an effort to show how globalization is a post-WW II concatenation of factors, many of which have their origin in the "peaceful" continuation of the "Allied" victories. Much of the technology making for increased compression of time and space, for the closer bonding that marks present-day globalization, can be found emerging at that time. Thus, where most students of the Cold War treat it as a traditional conflict in international relations, I approach it as a factor in the "making" of globalization.

Multinational corporations and non-governmental organizations are major actors in this new globalization phase. I also refer to them as "factors." Whatever term we use, the MNCs and NGOs must be placed alongside more traditional nation-states and international organizations as players in the globalization process. The challenge is not so much to see how they displace the nation-state, but how they seek to deal with the gaps opened up in governance by the new forces surging over the previous barriers. First, of course, we need a clear idea of the new, or newly enlarged, actors. Then we can speculate on what actual power they have, how they employ such power, with what possible outcomes, etc. To understand them, I have suggested that it is important to "map" them, i.e., to give visual representation to their existence and manifestations.

In my view the most important aspect of globalization, at least in long-range terms, is the change in consciousness that the process represents. It offers another identity alongside that of existing national, ethnic, and religious ones. It is the identity of being a human being, whose existence may be local but whose development increasingly is in global terms. Noting that the local and the global are intertwined, I call attention to the emergence of the concept of Humanity as the prime constituent of political, economic, social, and cultural measures and legislation. Cosmopolitanism can be said to have taken on a native habitat, a reality to match the inspirations and aspirations of earlier thinkers. Now it is more an empirical subject for historians and anthropologists than for theorizing by philosophers.[14]

In the last four chapters I pursue the moral implications of globalization. The first is an analysis of the way globalization is creating a global civil society, but how this is being hijacked at the present moment by forces that can be labeled as Global Islam and Global America. This is the most "political" of my chapters. The three that follow explore in much detail the way the "global" may tend to be more moral than the "local" in numerous situations. This runs against the received wisdom. I try to pursue this theme in detail, extending it to the debate about universals and the nature of science and human rights as forms of universal knowledge. Finally, I probe more deeply into how the concept of "Humanity" emerged from the events of WW II and the trials and tribunals of the subsequent half century. In the process, globalization can be said to be producing Humanity as a reality as well as a reification.

(4)

I want now in conclusion to set out two theses. Each is separate but related to the other, either directly or by affinity. Together and separately they are speculative extrapolations from the globalization hitherto described in the chapters of this book.

The first thesis compares present-day globalization to the French Revolution. It was the events of 1789 and the consequent Napoleonic extension of their implications that marked a major watershed in Western history, with significant ripples beyond. The French Revolution destroyed the privileges of the existing elites—nobility, clergy, and urban oligarchy—in short, the structure of feudalism. It broke down barriers to change of existing legal and political institutions. It furthered the confiscation of Church lands, as Henry VIII had done earlier in England, placing them on the market. It ended the restrictions of the guilds, abolished the sale of offices, and preached a radical form of equality. Spreading to other lands, with its armies based on universal military conscription sweeping all before it, it spread its reforms widely.

In the process, the Revolution prepared the way for economic and social growth of an extraordinary nature. It facilitated the spread of another revolution, industrialization, freeing up entrepreneurial energies and a spirit of innovation previously blocked by the old regimes and their institutions. It strongly secularized the societies in which it made its way, and in place of religion offered nationalism as the new faith and identity. It made the nation-state the reigning deity, and sought to place all interests in its service.

Now little of this happened all at once, or in the totally consistent fashion I have suggested.[15] Remnants of the feudal and old regime systems remained, reactions and restorations took place, and the changes that had taken place were on a West/East slope, with the Atlantic countries, in general, more advanced in this regard than those farther to the East. Nevertheless, the Revolution was widely heralded as a true break—a rupture—with the past. Welcomed by many, deplored by many others, the Revolution is an acknowledged fact. It transcended existing boundaries, broke down long-standing barriers between people, and peoples, and made for greater connections and dependencies between them. It can obviously be seen as a step toward greater globalization.[16]

I want to argue that it can also serve as a template for the latter in its present-day form. The details are certainly different. The nation-state, at the heart of the French Revolution, is being breached by the MNCs and NGOs of globalization. The state's centrality and sovereignty are having to be shared by a host of other contenders, of both an international and a global form. The Industrial Revolution, fostered by the French Revolution, has been superseded by the information revolution. The ocean as the conduit of power is being rivaled by space. The compression of space and time to be found at the end of the eighteenth century and into the nineteenth has been accelerated in a truly revolutionary fashion.

To summarize, then, my first thesis is that present-day globalization is the counterpart for our time of that earlier French Revolution. Both have removed reigning institutions and the holders of authority within them, and opened the way for new configurations of power and sovereignty. Both have shattered existing barriers and transcended identities and boundaries in a novel manner. The French Revolution's way was through violence, that of globalization by mainly economic and technological means. In the end, however, the way of globalization is of greater force and extent than that of its predecessor. If the Revolution had a major impact on many of its immediate neighbors, the present-day globalization process is worldwide in its effects. All peoples are actors, in principle and increasingly in practice, in this transforming historical experience. If anything, the twentieth-century rupture is more extensive and expansive than its earlier prototype.

My second thesis asserts that a profound change in categories has been taking place. For about three hundred years, something called Modernity reigned. It was the prime mode in which all sorts of people have tried to understand their position in time and society. In the last 50 years of the second millennium, however, a shift has occurred. Now, globalization has become the dominant mode of framing issues and questions. The process plays itself out in field after field. It is another element in the rupture that characterizes our time.

I will touch ever so briefly on a few of the elements in the shift of categories. The nation-state dominated in the thought-world of Modernity. Today, it is being transcended both in fact and in theory. Science seemed a relatively uncomplicated matter in the age of Modernity. It has now taken on new dimensions, embracing chaos and uncertainty while still retaining its hold on scientific method and thus universality in our time of globalization. Other such shifts—regarding religion, industry, and identity—have been mentioned earlier. To avoid losing sight of the forest for the trees, i.e., offering further details, I will simply here reassert without further ado my thesis that the categories of thought with which we approach our present experiences are becoming more and more those of globalization rather than those of modernity.[17]

(5)

In sum, our knowledge world is changing as rapidly as the material and social world around us. Globalization is as much a matter of soul and spirit as of body and boundaries. I have tried to treat both spheres in the course of saying what New Global History is, and is not. As I am presenting it, New Global History is both a continuation of and a rupture with other ways of knowing. It is also a challenge, which I am asking the reader to confront as impartially and boldly as possible. It requires us to step out into a new space and time, in response to the compressions of both that have taken place around us, and that are changing our world into a (new) global one. While the prospect may be scary, the promise is breath taking. In any case, we really have no choice other than about the ways in which we go forth to meet the challenge of our epoch.

Notes

Introduction

1 The deep-seated hostility among those who hold traditional political power to acknowledge the changed situation still obscures the gathering awareness of what is happening. Thus, a few years back, the current United States Secretary of State wrote how we must shun the idealism and moralism of impractical and naïve thinkers and actors, and conduct international relations "from the firm ground of the national interest, not from the interests of an illusory international community" (Condoleezza Rice, "Promoting the National Interest," *Foreign Affairs*, 79 (January/February 2000), 62. I came across this statement (which I owe to my friend Erez Manela) as I was finishing this book. New Global History deals not only with a so-called "illusory international community," but also with an equally "illusory global society." Rice's view, of course, is in tune with denying the reality of global warming, of disdaining to consult "foreign," i.e., international, legal systems, of not reckoning soberly with the diminution of national sovereignty in a globalizing world, etc. In the end, of course, the question is who is suffering from illusions. This book ends up trying to clarify that issue.

2 One of the earliest efforts to redeem contemporary history from the dustbin of the present, so to speak, is Geoffrey Barraclough, *An Introduction to Contemporary History* (London: C.A. Watts & Co., 1964). Due to Barraclough's effort and that of some others, contemporary history has reclaimed a modicum of respectability, much as it had with Herodotus, the founder of the inquiry known as history. Barraclough, incidentally, is a good starting point for reflections on world and global history.

3 While interest in the topic appears to be growing, it is generally approached in terms of philosophy or political science and not that of New Global History. See, for example, Heather Widdows, "Global Ethics: Foundations and Methodologies," in *Global Ethics and Civil Society*, ed. John Eades and Darren O'Byrne (Aldershot, UK: Ashgate, 2005).

1 Globalization without end

1 Melvin Richter, "Conceptualizing the Contestable: 'Begriffsgeschichte' and Political Concepts," in *Archiv für Begriffsgeschichte*, ed. Erich Rothaker (Hamburg: Felix Meiner Verlag, 2000), 138.

2 C. A. Bayly, " 'Archaic' and 'Modern' Globalization in the Eurasian and African Arena, c. 1750–1850," in *Globalization in World History*, ed. A. G Hopkins (Pimlico: London, 2002), 48–49.

3 Sylvia Walby, "The Myth of the Nation-state: Theorizing Society and Politics in a Global Era," *Sociology*, vol. 37, no. 3 (2003), 5.

4 A new and nuanced way of viewing the Treaty of Westphalia and its significance can be found in Benno Teschke, "Theorizing the Westphalian System of States: International Relations from Absolutism to Capitalism," *European Journal of International Relations*, vol. 8, no. 1 (2002). Cf. Adam David Morton, "The Age of Absolutism: Capitalism, the Modern States-system and International Relations," *Review of International Studies* (2005), 31.

5 James C. Scott, *Seeing Like a State: How Certain Schemes to Improve the Human Condition Have Failed* (New Haven: Yale University Press, 1998), takes up some of these developments in terms of the modern state's project of rendering society "legible" through various initiatives involving standardization and simplification, with the aim of improved taxation and control of the population so as to strengthen the nation's war-making powers. While the argument is tendentious, Scott does a good job of illuminating the ways in which the state became more and more powerful before the advent of present-day globalization. For a useful discussion of his book and its limitations, see the three review essays in *The American Historical Review*, vol. 106, no. 1 (February 2001), 106–29.

6 Martin Van Creveld, *The Rise and Decline of the State* (Cambridge: Cambridge University Press, 1999), 40. Creveld's observation that empires cannot accept equals is worth remembering when we come to Chapter 6, "The hijacking of global society."

7 Thomas A. Brady, Jr., "The Rise of Merchant Empires, 1400–1700," in *The Political Economy of Merchant Empires*, ed. James D. Tracy (Cambridge: Cambridge University Press, 1991), 119.

8 Giles Milton, *Samurai William* (New York: Farrar, Straus and Giroux, 2002), 10. Such a history would also have to be told in terms of the non-Western parts of the world and their contribution to the early globalization process. The reexamination especially of fifteenth-century Chinese and Indian history is vital to this effort. World historians are in a favorable situation to engage on this comparative task.

9 For details, see my chapter "Terms" in *Palgrave Advances in World History*, ed. Marnie Hughes-Warrington (New York: Palgrave Macmillan, 2005).

10 *Globalization in World History*, ed. A. G. Hopkins (Pimlico: London, 2002), 3.

11 Elizabeth Elbourne, "Word Made Flesh: Christianity, Modernity, and Cultural Colonialism in the Work of Jean and John Comarofff," *American Historical Review*, vol. 108, no. 2 (April 2003), 438.

12 See, for example, Kevin O'Rourke and Jeffrey G. Williamson, *Globalization and History: The Evolution of a Nineteenth-century Atlantic Economy* (Cambridge: MIT Press, 1999).

13 Ulrich Beck, "From Industrial Society to the Risk Society," *Theory, Culture & Society*, vol. 9, no. 1 (February 1992), 102. The next quote is from p. 98.

2 Onwards and outwards

1 Karl Marx and Frederick Engels, *Collected Works*, Vol. 6, 1845–8 (New York: International Publishers, 1976), 345.

2 Max Weber, *The Protestant Ethic and the Spirit of Capitalism*, tr. Talcott Parsons (New York: Charles Scribner's Sons, 1958), 13 and 17.

3 Quoted in Albert O. Hirschman, *The Passions and the Interests* (Princeton, NJ: Princeton University Press, 1977), 74, fn. b.

4 G. Barraclough, *An Introduction to Contemporary History* (London: C.A. Watts

& Co., 1964), has already been mentioned as an early work leading up to the promised land of global history. Michael Geyer and Charles Bright, "World History in a Global Age," *The American Historical Review*, vol. 100, no. 4, (October 1995), 1034–60, come close to crossing the boundary between world history, traditionally conceived, and what I am calling New Global History. Their ambivalence is reflected in their title. The article also offers a valuable bibliography. See also William H. McNeill, "The Changing Shape of World History," *History and Theory* Theme Issue 34 "World Historians and Their Critics," 14.

5 Manuel Castells, *The Rise of the Network Society*, Vol. I *The Information Age: Economy, Society and Culture* (Oxford: Blackwell Publishers, 1996), 92.

6 One of the earliest statements of this fact is Wolf Schafer's "Das 20. Jahrhundert hat gerade erst begonnen: Nach welchen Kriterien kann die Gegenwartsgeschichte periodisiert, kann eine Epoche konstruiert werden?" *Die Zeit*, 25 October 1996, 56. Even earlier, in 1993, in my Introduction to *Conceptualizing Global History*, ed. Bruce Mazlish and Ralph Buultjens (Boulder: Westview Press), I had used the term, but my colleague Wolf Schafer's article spells out in much greater detail the case for the suggested new periodization.

7 Quoted in Charles Coulston Gillespie, *Genesis and Geology* (Cambridge, MA: Harvard University Press, 1951), 104.

8 E. H. Carr, *What Is History?* (London: Penguin, 1961), 199.

9 An interesting book in this regard is Peter N. Stearns, *Global Outrage: The Impact of World Opinion on Contemporary History* (Oxford: Oneworld, 2005).

10 See, for example, Karl Moore and David Lewis, *Birth of the Multinational: 2000 Years of Ancient Business History—From Ashur to Augustus* (Copenhagen: Copenhagen Business School Press, 1999).

11 The new atlas, *Global Inc.* (New York: New Press, 2003), is accompanied by a digitized version allowing for constant responses to changing data, and a CD-ROM. *Leviathans: Multinational Corporations and New Global History*, ed. A. Chandler and B. Mazlish (Cambridge: Cambridge University Press, 2005) is based on the papers delivered at the conference, which underlay the mapping part of the project, plus others commissioned subsequently.

12 Here is where anthropologists might be able to use their special skills. Why not embed an anthropologist with a particular UN deployment, say in Kosovo or Darfur, and have him/her study in what ways, if any, the global commitment of these troops works in regard to their national origins. Is a sense of belonging to a larger-than-national military force present, and, if so, how does it manifest itself?

13 For more on glocalization and globalization generally, see Roland Robertson, *Globalization: Social Theory and Global Culture* (London: Sage, 1992). Robertson was and remains one of the earliest and most thoughtful sociologists to try to theorize the subject of globalization.

3 Cold War and globalization

1 Karl Jaspers, *Vom Ursprung und Ziel der Geschichte*, quoted in Martin Albrow, *The Global Age* (Stanford: Stanford University Press, 1997), 75.

2 A project seeking to deepen our understanding of Humanity as a concept emerging operationally out of WW II (philosophically, of course, there were predecessors) and as a tradition to be found in pre-WW II societies such as China, India, etc. is now underway. It is under the guidance of Zhong Longxi (City University of Hong Kong), Jorn Rusen (University of Bielefeld) and Bruce Mazlish (MIT).

3 For an interesting and provocative treatment of this development see Peter

Gowan, *The Global Gamble: Washington's Faustian Bid for World Dominance* (London: Verso, 1999).

4 Cf. Chapter 6, "The Hijacking of Global Society."

5 For an extensive treatment of this aspect of *Homo sapiens*, see my book *The Fourth Discontinuity: The Co-evolution of Humans and Machines* (New Haven: Yale University Press, 1993). The thinking in that book stands in back of much of what I am saying here, although in a different vein.

6 An early and classic treatment of this space race is Walter A. McDougall, *The Heavens and the Earth: A Political History of the Space Age* (New York: Basic Books, 1985). It must be noted that nationalism did not fully retreat from outer space. When the American flag was planted on the moon, it was an anachronism, recalling the placing of flags on earth sites such as the New World in the fifteenth century and the South Sea islands in the eighteenth century. More ominous today are the plans, especially by the USA, to "militarize" space.

7 Extremely useful in understanding these developments is Manuel Castells, *The Rise of the Network Society*, op. cit.

8 Quoted in Matthew Connelly, *A Diplomatic Revolution: Algeria's Fight for Independence and the Origins of the Post-Cold War Era* (Oxford: Oxford University Press, 2002), 27.

9 Quoted in the very interesting article by Fernando Coronil, "Towards a Critique of Globalcentrism: Speculations on Capitalism's Nature," *Public Culture* vol. 12, no. 2, (2000), 359. His argument, as he explains, is that "dominant discourses of globalization constitute a circuitous modality of Occidentalism that operates through the occlusion rather than the affirmation of the radical difference between the West and its Others," p. 354. For anyone interested in the question of whether globalization is simply a new form of imperialism, Coronil's article is essential reading; it also offers an astute qualification to my analysis of globalization. In the end, however, he softens his criticism and declares that: "A critique that demystifies globalization's universalistic claims but recognizes its liberatory potential may make less tolerable capitalism's destruction of nature and degradation of human lives and, in the same breath, expand the spaces where alternative visions of humanity are imagined." (370) Another article by Coronil, "Beyond Occidentalism: Toward Nonimperial Geohistorical Categories," *Cultural Anthropology*, vol. 11, no. 1 (Feb. 1996), offers an important reading of the effects of globalization on the self. His is a voice that needs very much to be heard in the debates over globalization. A relevant article is my own "Edward Said: The Colonial Spirit in a Globalizing World," *The Discourse of Sociological Practice*, vol. 7, nos. 1 and 2 (Spring/Fall 2005).

10 Cf. Charles S. Maier, "The Collapse of Communism: Approaches for a Future History," *History Workshop Journal*, vol. 31 (1991), 34–59.

11 An interesting account is given in Pankaj Mishra, "The Real Afghanistan," *New York Review of Books*, March 10, 2005, 44–8.

12 Such a dedication is generally attributed to Woodrow Wilson. As Erez Manela of Harvard University points out, however, Wilson's own initial draft of Article III "diluted the concept of inviolable sovereignty to the point of irrelevance." In the final text, as incorporated in Article X, the "preservation, even freezing, of the international status-quo" was reinstated by other hands. I owe this illumination of Wilson's actual position, and the quotes supporting it, to a personal communication from Professor Manela as well as to his article "A Man ahead of His Time?," *International Journal* (Autumn 2005).

13 Quoted in Stephen Jay Gould, "Darwin and Paley Meet the Invisible Hand," *Natural History*, vol. 11 (1990), p. 8.

14 Quoted in Fania Oz-Salzberger, "Civil Society in the Scottish Enlightenment," in *Civil Society: History and Possibilities*, ed. Sudipta Kaviraj and Sunil Khilnani (Cambridge: Cambridge University Press, 2001), 69–70.
15 Cf. Kaviraj and Khilnani, 72–3.

4 The multinational corporations

1 The extreme of such claims in regard to MNCs is to be found in Karl Moore and David Lewis, *Birth of the Multinational: 2000 Years of Ancient Business History—From Ashur to Augustus* (Copenhagen: Copenhagen Business School Press, 1999), previously mentioned. Though I have reservations about their thesis, the book is nevertheless an interesting and important contribution to the history of its subject.
2 For a visual representation of this almost J-shaped curve, see *Global Inc. An Atlas of the Multinational Corporations* (New York: New Press, 2003). In back of this chapter stands a project of the NGH initiative, which was to "Map the MNCs." In order to truly understand their importance we must "see" the history and present extent of the MNCs visually as well as mentally. If we open the usual atlas, we immediately see the world as depicted in terms of nation-states and empires—their boundaries, internal features, etc. With MNCs becoming the equal in power of many nation-states, for example, it is now necessary to show this by means of maps, bar graphs and other mapping devices; similarly we must represent the way the MNCs are transcending "natural" boundaries. In short, we must see the world globally as well as think it so. In the effort to prepare the way for the mapping—what should be mapped? how were the MNCs to be defined?, etc.—a conference was held, where commissioned papers were delivered. On their basis, as remarked in an earlier footnote, a volume has been published as a companion to *Global Inc.*, called *Leviathans: Multinational Corporations and the New Global History*, ed. Alfred D. Chandler, Jr. and Bruce Mazlish (Cambridge: Cambridge University Press, 2005). Here can be found the fuller story and analysis of the modern MNCs upon which this present chapter is built. Indeed, one of the chapters is on "A Global Elite?," where, for example, a detailed analysis of the attendees of a typical Davos gathering can be found. Incidentally, the whole mapping of the MNCs project should be viewed as an illustration of how the New Global History operates and brings its perspective to bear on concrete issues of globalization.
3 For a challenge to the general thesis that I am presenting as to the power of the MNCs, see Paul N. Doremus, Louis W. Pauly, Simon Reich, and William Keller, eds., *The Myth of the Global Corporation* (Princeton: Princeton University Press, 1999).
4 In the USA at least they are now treated as legal "persons." In the eyes of many this is a very harmful fiction. See, for example, Thom Hartmann, *Unequal Protection: The Rise of Corporate Dominance and the Theft of Human Rights* (Rodale, 2002), which, though popular in intent, is an informed treatment. For a more scholarly and historical approach see Pauline Maier, "The Revolutionary Origins of the American Corporation," *The William and Mary Quarterly*, 3rd Series, vol. 1, no. 1 (January 1993).
5 Cf. Peter Gowan, op. cit.
6 See *Leviathans*, op. cit., chapter 6.

5 The NGOs movement

1 See, for example, Lester M. Salamon's article in *Foreign Affairs*, vol. 73, no. 4 (July/August 1994), for alternative language.

2 Michael Edwards, *Civil Society* (Cambridge, UK: Polity, 2004), 21 and 17. It should be clear from what follows that I often use the term NGO as a generic term despite its variants.

3 Oddly enough, it appears that the Chinese government is actively encouraging the organization of particular NGOs, especially in regard to the environment! This must be treated, however, as the exception that proves the rule.

4 I am in debt to my colleague in the NGH project to map the NGOs, George Thomas, for much of what is said here and for further enlightenment on the subject of NGOs. Needless to say, both he and I are indebted to numerous other scholars and thinkers who have been working on the topic.

5 On the Salvation Army, see Harald Fischer-Tiné's contribution to the planned but as yet unpublished volume *Alternative Visions of World Order: Global Moments and Movements, 1880s–1930s*, ed. Sebastian Conrad and Dominic Sachsenmaier.

6 *Constructing World Culture: International Nongovernmental Organizations since 1875*, ed. John Boli and George M. Thomas (Stanford: Stanford University Press, 1999), 14.

7 Interestingly, as Boli and Thomas also tell us, "The shape of the growth curve for IGOs over the last hundred years is very similar to that of INGOs, although there are far fewer IGOs." (*Constructing World Culture*, 28). All of which suggests that the same pattern of growth of institutions responding to the process of globalization, of which they are part, can be found in many forms and areas. (Incidentally, at another point Boli and Thomas announce that "Since 1850 more than 35,000 private, not-for-profit organizations with an international focus have debuted on the world stage" (20), thus seeming to confuse our earlier cited figures. In concluding this note I might mention that Akira Iriye has a chart showing the expansion of INGOs from 5 in 1860 via steady rises to 1321 in 1960, 2725 in 1972 and 12,686 in 1984. More specifics will help to reconcile these figures.

8 For example, in *Civil Society in the Middle East*, ed. Augustus Richard Norton, vol. 1 (Leiden: E.S. Brill, 1995), we are told that Arab NGOs grew from about 20,000 in the mid-1960s to 70,000 in the late 1980s (39). Among the 70,000, Egypt accounted for about 20,000, but we are then informed that most of these were inactive or only moderately active (41). Earlier we have been told that Tunisian NGOs grew from 3,300 in 1988 to 5,100 in 1994 (18). How these NGOs interacted with INGOs, if at all, remains unknown. All of which further illustrates the difficulties in establishing global figures and the shape of the NGO movement worldwide.

9 William Korey, *NGOs and the Universal Declaration of Human Rights: "A Curious Grapevine"* (New York: St. Martin's Press, 1998), 29.

10 Paul Gordon Lauren, *The Evolution of International Human Rights: Visions Seen* (Philadelphia: University of Pennsylvania Press, 1998). A second edition appeared in 2003, with minor but significant emendations and additions. The quote given is from this edition, page 3. Lauren's is an historical treatment. A more philosophical one, of great worth, is Norberto Bobbio, *The Age of Rights*, tr. Allan Cameron (Cambridge, UK: Polity Press, 1996; orig. Italian, 1990).

11 *Managing Global Issues: Lessons Learned*, ed. P.J. Simmons and Chantal de Jonge Oudratt (Washington, DC: Carnegie Endowment for International Peace, 2001), 428. The author is Dinah L. Shelton, and her entire chapter is a valuable source.

12 Korey, op. cit., 2.
13 The classic treatment of Orientalism is the book by that name by Edward W. Said (New York: Vintage Books, 1979). His account shows how Western scholars painted the peoples of the "Orient" as not just different but inhuman.
14 Simmons and Oudratt, op. cit., 8.
15 Cf. *International Crimes, Peace, and Human Rights: The Role of the International Criminal Court*, ed. Dinah Shelton (Ardsley, NY: Transaction Publishers, 2000), xiv.
16 At one stage the Clinton administration in the US was prepared to go along with the agreement, but then reneged.
17 See, for example, *The Economist*, October 23, 2004.
18 See Clifford Bob, *The Marketing of Rebellion: Insurgents, Media, and International Activism* (Cambridge: Cambridge University Press, 2005). Bob offers as case studies the Nigerian Ogoni Movement and the Mexican Zapatista Uprising. For those who favor an activist approach to NGOs over an analytical one (I see a need for both), this book will take its place next to Margaret E. Keck and Kathryn Sikkink, *Activists beyond Borders* (Ithaca: Cornell University Press, 1998), along with others. In fact, of course, Bob's book, along with Keck and Sikkink's, is itself an analytical work, to be put in the service of activism. At the farthest end of his work, one might attribute to the "brand name" INGOs an indecent effort to take over the work on the ground and nullify its potentially rebellious nature; I myself do not read Bob in this manner.
19 See, for example, Andrew Dobson, "Globalisation, Cosmopolitanism and the Environment," *International Relations*, vol. 19, no. 3 (2005). As a follow-up, Dobson has written another article, "Thick Cosmopolitanism" (to be published in *Political Studies*, 2006), where he argues that there is a motivational vacuum at the heart of the cosmopolitan underpinnings of globalization, and that this must be filled by material connections in order that people will act in a just manner.
20 See, for example, Hartmut Rosa, "The Speed of Global Flows and the Pace of Democratic Politics," *New Political Science*, vol. 27, no. 4 (December 2005). An article such as this, of course, must be read in conjunction with the wide literature that deals with the relation of globalization to democracy. Among others, the writings of David Held and his colleagues figure prominently.
21 A fundamental work on the history of civil society is Jean L. Cohen and Andrew Arato, *Civil Society and Political Theory* (Cambridge: The MIT Press, 1992). The first few pages of Warren Breckman, *Marx, the Young Hegelians, and the Origins of Radical Social Theory: Dethroning the Self* (Cambridge: Cambridge University Press, 1999), are a very suggestive treatment of this part of the concept's history. The direction in which Breckman takes his work can be found in his statement that "the question of civil society was, as it still is today, essentially related to the question of the nature of sovereignty; and this question in turn devolved upon a more basic question about the nature of the self in its manifold roles as 'sovereign,' 'citizen,' and 'subject'." (5).
22 Jan Aart Scholte, *Democratizing the Global Economy: The Role of Civil Society* (first published 2003 by the Centre for the Study of Globalisation and Regionalism, University of Warwick), 2.
23 Helmut K. Anheier, *Civil Society: Management, Evaluation, Policy* (London: Earthscan, 2004), 20.
24 Quoted in Anheier, 20. Habermas's exciting and fundamental work in this regard is *The Structural Transformation of the Public Sphere: An Inquiry into a Category of Bourgeois Society*, tr. Thomas Burger with the assistance of Frederick Lawrence (Cambridge: The MIT Press, 1991; orig. Ger. 1962).

25 See, for example, *Civil Society in the Muslim World*, ed. Amyn B. Sajoo (London: I.B. Tauris Publishers, 2002), a publication in cooperation with the London Institute of Ismaili Studies, and *Civil Society in the Middle East*, ed. Norton, op. cit. An especially interesting collection is Kaviraj and Khilnani, eds., op. cit., which combines secular, Western, Muslim and other points of view in an overall treatment of its subject.

26 Thomas Metzger, "The Western Concept of the Civil Society in the Context of Chinese History," Hoover Institution, Hoover Essay (see the website http://www-hoover.stanford.edu/publications/he/21/a.html).

6 The hijacking of global society

1 *Global Civil Society 2003*, ed. Mary Kaldor, Helmut Anheier, and Marlies Glasius (Oxford: Oxford University Press, 2003), 4.

2 Martin Shaw, "The Global Transformation of the Social Sciences," in Ibid., 44.

3 For a similar view, see John Keene, "Global Civil Society?," in *Global Civil Society 2001*, ed. Helmut Anheier, Marlies Glasius and Mary Kaldor (Oxford: Oxford University Press, 2001), 32. The point still remains arguable, however, in certain circles, where MNCs are excluded from being a part of civil society.

4 For a renewed defense of cosmopolitanism in the global epoch, see Kwame Anthony Appiah, *Cosmopolitanism: Ethics in a World of Strangers* (New York: W.W. Norton, 2006).

5 Mary Kaldor, "A Decade of Humanitarian Intervention: The Role of Global Civil Society," in *Global Civil Society 2001*, op. cit., 109.

6 Mary Kaldor, Helmut Anheier, and Marlies Glasius, "Global Civil Society in an Era of Regressive Globalisation," in *Global Civil Society 2003*, op. cit., 5.

7 Cf. Edward Luther Stevenson, *Terrestrial and Celestial Globes*, 2 vols. (New Haven: Yale University Press, 1921).

8 Mehdi Mozaffari, "Bin Laden: Terrorism and Islamism," paper published by Department of Political Sciences, Aarhus University, Denmark, 2001.

9 For Khomeini and his sense of humiliation, see Bruce Mazlish, "The Hidden Khomeini," in *The Leader, the Led, and the Psyche* (Hanover: Wesleyan University Press, 1990). For the fatwa of February 23, 1998, see Osama Bin Laden, available at http://jihadunspun.com/Bin Ladens-Network/statements/jajac.html.

10 For example, as Mohammad Arkoun, "Locating Civil Society in Islamic Contexts," in *Civil Society in the Muslim World*, ed. A. B. Sajoo (London: I. B. Taurus Publishers, 2002), remarks about the challenge of modernity and its institutions, it will be difficult to deal with "as long as the state remains patrimonial and social mentalities are shaped by patriarchal kinship mechanisms" (p. 43).

11 Among the works looking at modernity and globalization in the Arab world, see, for example, Olivier Roy, *Globalised Islam* (London: Hurst, 2004), Clement M. Henry and Robert Springborg, *Globalization and the Politics of Development* (Cambridge: Cambridge University Press, 2001), and Faisal Devji, *Landscapes of the Jihad: Militancy, Morality, Modernity* (Ithaca: Cornell University Press, 2005). Pankaj Mishra, reviewing a number of books in the *New York Review of Books*, summarizes how radical Islam arose from the events of Afghanistan, where the joint training and fighting bound Islamists together, in what has become "the first global jihad in Islam's long history" (November 17, 2005, 15).

12 *New Yorker*, March 29, 2004.

13 See the *New York Times*, April 26, 2004, 7.

14 Peter Gowan, op. cit., ix.
15 Cf. Martin Shaw, *Theory of the Global State* (Cambridge: Cambridge University Press, 2000).
16 *National Security Strategy of the United States of America*. Available at http://www.whitehouse.gov/nsc/nss.html.
17 To further explore this paradox, a conference was held at Yale University in October 2003, the result of a collaboration between the Yale Center for the Study of Globalization and the New Global History Initiative. The resultant volume is being published by Stanford University Press.
18 NSS, 2002, p. i, Section 1.
19 P. Boyer, "General Clark's Battles," *New Yorker*, November 17, 2003, 80.
20 *New York Times*, November 13, 2002. Subsequently, Rove claimed he was misquoted, and that the question concerned 200,000 Americans who marched in Washington protesting the war. Given Rove's track record in manipulating the news, the original quote seems plausible; correct or not it gets at the truth symbolically.
21 Carl Bowman, "Survey Report: the Evidence for Empire," *The Hedgehog Review*, vol. 5, no. 3 (2003), 78 and 74.

7 The global and the local

1 Max Weber, *Economy and Society*, ed. Guenther Roth and Claus Wittich, 2 vols. (Berkeley: University of California Press, 1978), Vol. I, 637.
2 Roland Robertson, *Globalization* (London: Sage, 1992), 173–4. It is significant that Robertson credits the Japanese with the first introduction of this term, and then urges us to "transcend the discourse of 'localism-globalism'."
3 I am in debt to Tadashi Yamamoto for alerting me to this example.
4 Furukawa Shun'ichi, "Decentralization in Japan," in *Japan's Road to Pluralism: Transforming Local Communities in the Global Era*, ed. Furukawa Shun'ichi and Manju Toshihiro, Chapter 1 (Tokyo: Japan Center for Economic Exchange, 2003), 23.
5 Sylvia Walby, "The Myth of the Nation-state: Theorizing Society and Politics in a Global Era," *Sociology* (2003) 37, no. 3, 531–48.
6 Cf. on these matters my book *A New Science: The Breakdown of Connections and the Birth of Sociology* (University Park, PA: Pennsylvania State University Press, 1993; orig. hardback, Oxford University Press, 1989).
7 Quoted in László Kontler, "Savages Noble and Ignoble. Civilisation and Race in George Forster's 'Voyage Round the World' (1777)", MS, 1.
8 Alexis de Tocqueville, *Democracy in America*, ed. J. P. Mayer, tr. George Lawrence (New York: Doubleday, 1969), 63.
9 Even with the end of formal slavery and segregation, the issue is still very much alive, as evinced in the Oklahoma City bombing in 1996 by Timothy McVeigh. He is believed to have had ties to the Arizona Patriots and similar groups, who, we are told, "strenuously reject any form of government above the county level and specifically oppose federal and state income taxes, the existence of the Federal Reserve system and the supremacy of the federal judiciary over local courts" (Bruce Hoffman, *Inside Terrorism*, New York: Columbia University Press, 1998, 110.) The overlap in the USA of some of these attitudes with those encouraged, for example, by the Reagan administration is patent, showing not only that the local is alive and "well" but widespread.
10 Sophia Rosenfeld, "Citizens of Nowhere in Particular: Cosmopolitanism, Writing, and Political Engagement in Eighteenth-century Europe," *National*

Identities, vol. 4, no. 1 (March 2002), 25–43, is an excellent article in which to pursue some of the themes raised here about cosmopolitanism.

11 Quoted in Albert O. Hirschman, *The Passions and the Interests* (Princeton: Princeton University Press, 1977), 74.

12 Arjun Appadurai, *Modernity at Large: Cultural Dimensions of Globalization* (Minneapolis: University of Minnesota Press, 1996), 52, 64 and 57.

13 Bruce Robbins, *Secular Vocations* (London: Verso, 1993), 196–7.

14 Paul Rabinow, "Representations Are Social Facts," in *Writing Culture*, ed. James Clifford and George E. Marcus (Berkeley: University of California Press, 1986), 258.

15 Lila Abu-Lughod, "The Interpretation of Culture(s) after Television," *Representations*, no. 59 (Summer 1997), 121–3.

16 The quotations are in regard to Celia Applegate, *A Nation of Provincials: The German Idea of Heimat* (Berkeley: University of California Press, 1990), in an article, "The Vernacular International," by Maiken Umbach in *National Identities*, vol. 4, no. 1 (March 2002), 46.

17 Alon Confino and Ajay Skaria, "The Local Life of Nationhood," in ibid., 5.

18 See Maiken Umbach's review of Abigail Green, *Fatherlands: State-Building and Nationhood in Nineteenth-century Germany* (New York: Cambridge University Press, 2001), *Journal of Interdisciplinary History*, vol. xxxiii, no. 4 (Spring 2003), 648. As can readily be seen, there is something of a cottage industry in regard to this subject.

19 Edmund Burke, *Reflections on the Revolution in France*, ed. Thomas H. D. Mahoney (New York: The Liberal Arts Press, 1955), 53. As can be seen, I do not accept this statement as the final word on the subject.

20 *The Economist*, April 13, 2002 "A Special Survey of Television," p. 13.

21 *World Paper*, July 3, 2002.

22 A model study in this regard, though for an earlier period and a more restricted subject, is Thomas L. Haskell, "Capitalism and the Origins of the Humanitarian Sensibility," *American Historical Review*, vol. 90, nos. 2 and 3 (April and June 1985).

8 Toward a higher morality

1 Quoted in E. H. Gombrich, " 'They Were All Human Beings—So Much Is Plain': Reflections on Cultural Relativism in the Humanities," *Critical Inquiry*, vol. 13, no. 4 (Summer 1987), 687. I have not cited the original because I wanted to call attention to Gombrich's article as well.

2 Haskell, op. cit.

3 Sven Beckert, *The Monied Metropolis: New York City and the Consolidation of the American Bourgeoisie, 1850–1896* (Cambridge: Cambridge University Press, 1993). Incidentally, it was only natural that Beckert would then go on to write about cotton as a global commodity.

4 For more on this subject see my *The Uncertain Sciences* (New Haven: Yale University Press, 1998).

5 *New Yorker*, May 19, 2003, 56.

6 Christina Klein, *Cold-War Orientalism: Asia in the Middlebrow Imagination, 1945–1961* (Berkeley: University of California Press, 2003), 14.

7 See *A New Science*, op. cit.

8 To go further in thinking about humanity and its meaning, Professor Zhong Longxi of the City University of Hong Kong, Professor Jorn Rusen of Essen, Germany, and I are engaged in a project to investigate the way in which

"humanity" or its equivalent has been and is conceptualized and thought about in different cultures and societies.

9 For an excellent presentation of this view, see the previously mentioned article by Balmurli Natrajan, "Beyond Homogenization versus Heterogenization: Difference and Culture in Globalization," paper prepared for a conference on Globalization, Civil Society and Philanthropy at the Rockefeller Archive Center, June 5–7, 2003.

10 Ibid., 12.

11 Jürgen Habermas, *The Postnational Constellation*, tr. Max Pensky (Cambridge, MA: The MIT Press, 2001), 71.

9 Global Humanity

1 *New York Times*, July 4, 2003, A14.

2 For decades more or less forgotten, the Constantinople trials, held by the British in the shadow of the collapse of the Ottoman Empire, were a forerunner of the Nuremberg trials. In the Constantinople case, the British finally gave up, swayed in part by the fact that in order to capture the "criminals" British soldiers might be killed—a familiar story today with different names. Now the Turkish/Armenian question is returning with a vengeance. Part of the question is what to call the events of 1915: massacre, genocide, or what? Turkish nationalists reject the word "genocide." Armenians insist on it as the correct description of what happened. For a sense of the discourse, see, for example, the work of the historian Fatma Muge Gocek. An excellent treatment of the general topic of genocide is Eric D. Weitz, *A Century of Genocide: Utopias of Race and Nation* (Princeton: Princeton University Press, 2003), which starts with a short section; "An Armenian Prelude." Equally valuable is Gary Jonathon Bass, *Stay the Hand of Vengeance: The Politics of War Crimes Tribunals* (Princeton: Princeton University Press, 2000).

3 Cf. *International Crimes, Peace, and Human Rights: The Role of the International Criminal Court*, ed. Dinah Shelton (Ardsley, NY: Transnational Publishers, 2000), 39.

4 A comparison with what is said in Chapter 6, "The hijacking of global society," comes quickly to mind.

5 See Gerard Alexander, "The Realities of Confronting Genocide: A Review of Samantha Power's 'A Problem From Hell'," *The Hedgehog Review*, vol. 5, no. 1 (Spring 2003), 93. See also Power's book (New York: Basic Books, 2002). Cf. William Korey's account in *NGOs and the Universal Declaration of Human Rights*, op. cit.

6 Alexander, op. cit., 100.

7 For more on viewing the present-day process of globalization historically, as exemplified in the work of the New Global History initiative, see my introduction to *Conceptualizing Global History*, ed. B. Mazlish and R. Buultjens (Newton Center, MA: New Global History Press, 2003, a reprint of the original 1993 edition from Westview Press), and *The Global History Reader*, ed. Bruce Mazlish and Akira Iriye (London: Routledge, 2004). Further, see the website www.-newglobalhistory.org.

8 Quoted in Joan Acocella, "Blocked," *New Yorker*, June 14 and 21, 2004, 128.

9 The classic work is Arthur O. Lovejoy, *The Great Chain of Being* (Cambridge, MA: Harvard University Press 1953).

10 Cf. the account by Gunnar Broberg, "Homo sapiens. Linnaeus's Classification of Man," in *Linnaeus: The Man and His Work*, ed. Tore Frängsmyr (Berkeley: University of California Press, 1983), 176.

11 See entry for Humanity in *OED*.

12 For recent views on this subject, see *New York Times*, November 25, 2003.

13 Lynn Hunt, "The Psycho-cultural Origins of Human Rights," unpub. MS.

14 Ibid., 21.

15 Cf. Terry Pinkard, *Hegel: A Biography* (Cambridge: Cambridge University Press, 2000).

16 G. F. W. Hegel, *Philosophy of Right*, tr. T. M. Knox (Oxford: Clarendon Press, 1942) 134, #209.

17 For a fascinating effort to go beyond Hegel's Eurocentric definition of the conscious self, see Fernando Coronil, "Beyond Occidentalism: Toward Nonimperial Geohistorical Categories," *Cultural Anthropology*, vol. 11, no. 1 (Feb. 1996).

18 The quotation is from de Maistre's *Considérations sur la France* (1796).

19 Felipe Fernandez-Armesto, *Civilizations: Culture, Ambition, and the Transformation of Nature* (New York: The Free Press, 2001), 25. Cf. Jorn Rusen, "Human Rights from the Perspective of a Universal History," in *Human Rights and Cultural Diversity*, ed. Wolfgang Schmale (Goldbach: Keip Publishing, 1993). As Rusen formulates the issue, "Many of the names known to be used by groups to describe themselves—such as Apache, Comanche, Khoi-khoi, Egyptian, Bantu and Roma—in fact mean simply 'human being'. The quality of being a human being is, in other words, originally only ascribed to those who are a member of one's own social grouping." (41). In the last few centuries in the West, the word "civilized" tended to take the place of oneself being human and others not.

20 This is the charge made by Andrew Dobson in his thoughtful essay "Thick Cosmopolitanism," already mentioned as forthcoming in *Political Studies*, 2006. In fact, however, his call for material ties that bind as the basis for justice is exactly what parts of globalization are bringing about in increased measure. A very different type of criticism of the notion of Humanity can be found in Michel Foucault and fellow postmodernists (although Foucault denied that he was one). See Foucault's *The Order of Things: An Archaeology of the Human Sciences*, translator not given (New York: Vintage Books, 1973), especially Chapter 10.

Conclusion

1 Much of the type of work I am advocating takes place under the heading of historical sociology, or sociological history. This is one reason why some of the best articles and books of the kind I am arguing for can be found in sociological as well as historical journals.

2 An interesting attempt to point us in the right direction is Martin Shaw, "The Global Transformation of the Social Sciences," in Kaldor, Anheier, and Glasius, eds., op. cit. For further hints at my own ideas in this regard see the Introduction, Sections 3 and 5, to *The Global History Reader*, op. cit., as well as the readings therein.

3 See Martin W. Lewis and Kären E. Wigen, *The Myth of Continents: A Critique of Metageography* (Berkeley: University of California Press, 1997).

4 For my own contributions on these topics, see, for example, my chapter "Terms" in Hughes-Warrington, op. cit., as well as the article "Comparing Global History to World History," *Journal of Interdisciplinary History*, vol. 28, no. 3 (Winter 1998).

5 Webster's Dictionary for 1961 may be the site of the first appearance of the word "globalization." See, further, Richard Kilminster, "Globalization as an Emergent Concept," *The Limits of Globalization: Cases and Arguments*, ed. Alan Scott (London: Routledge, 1997), 257.

6 See George Steinmetz, "Return to Empire: The New U.S. Imperialism in Comparative Historical Perspective," *Sociological Theory*, vol. 23 (4 December 2005), for a comprehensive and incisive treatment of the subject and the distinction between colonialism and imperialism. A good short book is Jürgen Osterhammel, *Colonialism: A Theoretical Overview*, tr. from the German by Shelley L. Frisch (Princeton: Marcus Wiener Publishers, 1997). My review of this book, entitled "Colonialism: A Theoretical Overview," is in the *Journal of World History*, vol. 10, no. 1 (Spring 1999).

7 John Tomlinson, *Cultural Imperialism: A Critical Introduction* (Baltimore: Johns Hopkins University Press, 1991), is an excellent book with which to begin the inquiry.

8 On regionalism, see Peter J. Katzenstein, *A World of Regions: Asia and Europe in the American Imperium* (Ithaca: Cornell University Press, 2005).

9 Cf. the previously cited Balmurli Natrajan, "Beyond Homogenization versus Heterogenization: Difference and Culture in Globalization," paper prepared for a conference on Globalization, Civil Society and Philanthropy at the Rockefeller Archive Center, June 5–7, 2003.

10 Quotations are from the announcement of an International Summer Academy on Islam and the Repositioning of Religion, Essen, Germany, July 16–30, 2006. The conveners, to whom I refer as "one scholar," are Georg Stauth and Armando Salvatore. My interlocutor is the latter.

11 See the review-essay by Mary Louise Roberts in *History and Theory*, vol. 44, no. 3 (October 2005), 456. One exception to my generalization is Sasha Roseneil, "The Global Common: The Global, Local and Personal; Dynamics of the Women's Peace Movement in the 1980s," *The Limits of Globalization*, ed. Alan Scott (London: Routledge, 1997).

12 Ulrich Beck has been a leading figure in dealing with the subject of risk in globalization. See, for example, his "World Risk Society a Cosmopolitan Society? Ecological Questions in a Framework of Manufactured Uncertainties," *Theory, Culture & Society*, vol. 13, no. 4 (November 1996).

13 See Anna Lowenhaupt Tsing, *Friction: An Ethnography of Global Connection* (Princeton: Princeton University Press, 2005). The author is an ethnographer, who uses her discipline as an exciting means of exploring globalization.

14 Appiah, op. cit., appears to be the exception, with much to say of importance about its subject in a globalizing context.

15 See Arno J. Mayer, *The Persistence of the Old Regime: Europe to the Great War* (New York: Pantheon Books, 1981), for an important reminder of how the past lingers on.

16 The unpublished paper, still in draft, by Daron Acemoglu, Simon Johnson, and James Robinson, "Consequences of Radical Institutional Reform: The French Revolution," is most suggestive in this regard.

17 In another book, I hope to deal in detail with this momentous shift in categories of thought from modernity to globalization.

Index

Related titles from Routledge

The Enlightenment World
– New in Paperback
Martin Fitzpatrick, Peter Jones
and Christa Knellwolf

The Enlightenment World offers an informed, comprehensive and up-to-date analysis of the European Enlightenment (circa. 1720–1800) as both an historical epoch and a cultural formation. This prestigious collection begins with the intellectual origins of the Enlightenment, and spans early formations up to both contemporary and modern critics of the Enlightenment.

The chapters, written by leading international experts, represent the most cutting-edge research within the field and include:

- The High Enlightenment

- Polite Culture and the Arts

- Reforming the World

- Material and Pop Culture

- Transformations and Exploration.

Covering topics as diverse as government, fashion, craftsmen and artisans, philanthropy, cross-cultural encounters, feminism, censorship, science and education, this volume will provide essential reading for all students of the Enlightenment.

ISBN10: 0415–40408–8 (Pb)
ISBN13: 978–0–415–40408–2 (Pb)

Available at all good bookshops
For ordering and further information please visit:
www.routledge.com

Related titles from Routledge

Europe: A Cultural History
Second Edition
Peter Rietbergen

Following on from his highly acclaimed first publication, Peter Rietbergen's excellent second edition brings the reader up to date with Europe's current cultural trends.

Rietbergen examines the many varied cultural building blocks of Europe, their importance in the continent's cultural identity, and how the perception of Europe has changed over the centuries.

Working chronologically from the beginnings of agricultural society in Africa before Christ, right up to today's mass culture, the book studies culture through the media of literature, art, science, technology and music.

With thorough revisions on the late twentieth and early twenty-first century, a wide selection of excerpts, lyrics from contemporary songs, and illustrations, this book is an excellent student resource for both historical and cultural studies.

ISBN10: 0–415–32358–4 (Hb)
ISBN10: 0–415–32359–2 (Pb)

ISBN13: 978–0–415–32358–1 (Hb)
ISBN13: 978–0–415–32359–8 (Pb)

Related titles from Routledge

Christianity and Sexuality in the Early Modern World
Merry E. Wiesner-Hanks

In this lively and compelling study, Professor Wiesner-Hanks examines the ways in which Christian ideas and institutions shaped sexual norms and conduct from the time of Luther and Columbus to that of Thomas Jefferson. Providing a global overview, and including chapters on Protestant, Catholic and Orthodox Europe, Latin America, Africa, Asia and North America, this volume examines marriage, divorce, fornication, illegitimacy, clerical sexuality, witchcraft and love magic, homosexuality and moral crimes.

ISBN10: 0415–14433–7 (Hb)
ISBN10: 0–415–14434–5 (Pb)

ISBN13: 978–0–415–14433–9 (Hb)
SBN13: 978–0–415–14434–6 (Pb)

Available at all good bookshops
For ordering and further information please visit:
www.routledge.com

Related titles from Routledge

Religion and Society in Early Modern England: A Sourcebook

Second Edition

David Cressy and
Lori Anne Ferrell

'An accessible and extremely useful collection of primary source material ... an invaluable companion volume to textbooks on the long English Reformation' – Ecclesiastical History

Standing as the only book of this kind in its field, this second edition of a successful sourcebook now includes the latest research and provides students with an excellent overview and study of this important and complex period: the English Reformation.

Revised throughout, this book brings together a collection of sources, including narratives, reports, church documents and parliamentary proceedings. Here is presented the transformation of English religious culture from the 1530s to the 1660s, when the Roman Catholic Church was shattered and the Protestant Church of England established.

ISBN10: 0–415–34443–3 (Hb)
ISBN10: 0–415–34444–1 (Pb)

ISBN13: 978–0–415–34443–2 (Hb)
ISBN13: 978–0–415–34444–9 (Pb)

Available at all good bookshops
For ordering and further information please visit:

www.routledge.com